The Ultimate Air Fryer Bible [PART 1]

Cook and Taste Thousands of Fried Recipes, Save Your Money and Blow Your Friend's Mind. BONUS: 50+ Mediterranean Recipes

By

Michelle Polpetta

The trademarks that are used are without any consent, and the publication of the trademark is without permission or backing by the trademark owner. All trademarks and brands within this book are for clarifying purposes only and are the owned by the owners themselves, not affiliated with this document.

Table of Contents

The Healthy Air Fryer Cookbook with Pictures

The Complete Air Fryer Cookbook with Pictures

Air Fryer Cookbook for Two

The Mediterranean Diet Cookbook with Pictures

The Healthy Air Fryer Cookbook with Pictures

70+ Fried Tasty Recipes to Kill Hunger, Be Super Energetic and Make Your Day Brighter

By Michelle Polpetta

Table of Contents:

Introduction

An air fryer is a little kitchen appliance which imitates the outcomes of deep frying foods with the excess grease. As opposed to submerging food in order to fry it, the more food is put within the fryer together with a rather tiny quantity of oil. The food is subsequently "fried" having just hot air cooking. Food is cooked fast Because of the high heat and, because of the small quantity of oil onto the exterior of the meals, the outside will be emptied, like it was fried!

So, here we have discussed 70 best and healthy recipes for you that you can try at home and enjoy cooking using an air fryer.

Chapter 1: Air fryer Basics and 20 Recipes

Type of air fryer:

There're some air fryers that are over $300 and the one I used was less than a hundred. I didn't want you to splurge on the expensive one immediately because I was like what if I don't even use this thing? I want you to know that I'm going to use it first so I bought this for less than $100. This one is perfectly fine. It's big, it cooks a lot and it works just as good if not better than the more expensive models.

I'm going to bring you many air fryer recipes that are super easy. Even though it takes up quite a bit of counter space, it does a good job getting things crispy and delicious. Let's start with four recipes i.e. Bacon, Brussels sprouts, chicken wings and chicken breasts. So, let's get started.

1. **Air fryer Bacon Recipe**

I'm going to use four slices of bacon and I'm going to cut them in half on the cutting board.

So, here's the air fryer that I have:

It is a 5.7 quart which is a pretty large air fryer. You take out the drawer and then we're going to lay the bacon inside of the air fryer, as it all fits. You want it to be a single layer so that they get evenly cooked. We're going to put this back in so we set the temperature for 350 degrees and they will cook for about nine minutes. We will also check them a couple of times just to make sure they're not getting too overdone. That's all there is to it, so our air fryer bacon is already and let's pull it out.

If you wanted it a little crispy, you could leave it in for probably just one more minute but I like it like this.

2. Air Fryer Apple Pie Chips

Let us be honest: If you are craving super-crispy, crunchy apple chips, then baking them in the oven is not good for you. The air fryer, on the other hand, is best.

You'll begin by slicing an apple (any variety will probably work, although a red apple generates extra-pretty processors), and in case you've got a mandolin, utilize it as the thinner the slice, the crispier the processor. Toss the pieces with cinnamon and nutmeg, put an even coating into a preheated air fryer, coat with cooking spray, and stir fry until golden. You will have a tasty snack in under 10 minutes. For maximum crunchiness, let cool completely before eating.

Ingredients

- Moderate red apple

- 1/4 tsp ground nutmeg

- 1/2 tsp ground cinnamon

- Cooking spray

Instructions

- ❏ Thinly slice the apple into 1/8-inch-thick slices using a knife or rather on a mandoline.

❏ Toss the apple slices with 1/2 teaspoon ground cinnamon along with 1/4 teaspoon ground nutmeg.

❏ Preheat in an air fryer into 375ºF and place for 17 minutes. Coat the fryer basket with cooking spray. Put just one layer of apple pieces into a basket and then spray with cooking spray.

❏ Air fry until golden-brown, rotating the trays halfway through to keep the apples at level, about 7 minutes total.

❏ Allow the chips to cool entirely too crisp.

❏ Repeat with the air fryer for the remaining apple pieces.

3. **Air-fryer Chicken Wings**

We will get started on the chicken wings.

Ingredients:

- 12 Chicken wings

- Salt

- Pepper

Method:

I'm going to put them in the air fryer basket and then I'm going to season them with salt and pepper. I've got these all in a single layer and they're kind of snug in there which is fine because they're going to shrink as they cook.

I put in about 12 chicken wings fit in my air fryer basket and now we're going to cook them for 25 minutes at 380 degrees. What that's going to do is it really get them cooked and then we're going to bump up the temperature and we will get them crispy. The first cook on our wings is done and now we are going to put it back in the air fryer at 400 degrees for about three to five minutes to get them nice and crispy. With this recipe and most air fryer recipes, whenever you're cooking things for longer than I would say five minutes, you may want to pull the basket out and shake what's inside. It is to make sure that it gets evenly cooked and I like to do that about every five minutes. Our wings are done. Look at how good they look in there nice and crispy.

This took about three minutes as I didn't have to do the full five minutes for these.

4. **Air Fryer Mini Breakfast Burritos**

All these air-fried miniature burritos are fantastic to get a catch's go breakfast or perhaps to get a midday snack. Leave the serrano Chile pepper for a spicy version.

Ingredients

- 1 tablespoon bacon grease

- 1/4 cup Mexican-style chorizo

- 2 tbsp. sliced onion

- 1 serrano pepper, chopped

- salt and ground black pepper to taste

- 4 (8 inch) flour tortillas

- 1/2 cup diced potatoes

- 2 large eggs

- avocado oil cooking spray

Instructions

- ❖ Cook chorizo in an air fryer over medium-high heat, stirring often, until sausage operates into a dark crimson, 6 to 8 minutes.

- ❖ Melt bacon grease in precisely the exact way over medium-high warmth.

- ❖ Add onion and serrano pepper and continue stirring and cooking until berries are fork-tender, onion is translucent, and serrano pepper is tender in 2 to 6 minutes.

- ❖ Add eggs and chorizo; stir fry till cooked and fully integrated into curry mixture in about 5 minutes. Season with pepper and salt.

- ❖ Meanwhile, heat tortillas directly onto the grates of a gasoline stove until pliable and soft.

- ❖ Put 1/3 cup chorizo mixture down the middle of each tortilla.

❖ Fold top and bottom of tortillas over the filling, then roll into a burrito form. Mist with cooking spray and put in the basket of a fryer.

❖ Flip each burrito above, peppermint with cooking spray, and fry until lightly browned, 2 to 4 minutes longer.

5. Herb Chicken Breast

Now let's get to the herb chicken breast.

Ingredients

- Salt

- Pepper

- Chicken Breast

- Smoked Paprika

- Butter

Method:

We've got two chicken breasts. We've got butter, Italian seasoning salt, pepper and smoked paprika. We're going to mix all of that into the butter to give it a quick mix. Now we've got our two chicken breasts here and we're going to spread the mixture over each chicken breast to give it a nice flavorful crust.

Put these in the air fryer with some tongs. We're ready to cook these in the air fryer.

Cook them at 370 degrees for about 10 to 15 minutes and then check it with a meat thermometer to make sure that they're perfectly cooked. Because we don't want them to be overcooked, then they'll be dry and we definitely don't want them to be undercooked.

Okay, we pulled our chicken out of the air fryer. We had one chicken breast that was smaller so it came out a little bit earlier and now we have this one that's ready and its right at 165. So, we know that our chickens are not going to be dry. Let's cut into one of these. Those are perfectly cooked and juicy

6. Three Cheese Omelet

Ingredients

- 3 Tbsp. heavy whipping cream

- ½ tsp salt

- 4 eggs

- ¼ cup cheddar cheese, grated

- ¼ cup provolone cheese

- ¼ tsp ground black pepper

- ¼ cup feta cheese

Method:

❖ Preheat your air fryer to 350 degrees F and line a baking pan using parchment paper. Be sure the pan will fit on your fryer- normally a seven inch round pan will do the job flawlessly.

❖ In a small bowl, whisk together the eggs, cream, pepper and salt

❖ Pour the mixture into the prepared baking pan then place the pan on your preheated air fryer.

❖ Cook for approximately ten minutes or till the eggs are completely set.

❖ Sprinkle the cheeses round the boiled eggs and then return the pan into the air fryer for one more moment to melt the cheese.

7. Patty Pan Frittata

I had a gorgeous patty pan squash sitting on my counter tops and was wondering exactly what to do with this was fresh and yummy for my loved ones. I had not made breakfast however so a summer squash frittata appeared in order! Comparable to zucchini, patty pan squash leant itself well to my fundamental frittata recipe. Serve with your favorite brunch sides or independently. You could also cool and serve cold within 24 hours.

Ingredients

- 1 patty pan squash

- 1 tbsp. unsalted butter

- 4 large eggs

- 1/4 cup crumbled goat cheese

- 1/4 cup grated Parmesan cheese

- salt and ground black pepper to taste

- 1/4 cup

- 2 medium scallions, chopped, green and white parts split

- 1 tsp garlic, minced

- 1 small tomato, seeded and diced

- 1 tsp hot sauce, or to flavor

Instructions

❖ Press 5-inch squares of parchment paper to 8 cups of a muffin tin, creasing where essential.

❖ Heat butter over moderate heat; stir fry into patty pan, scallion whites, salt, garlic, and pepper. Transfer into a bowl and set aside.

❖ Add sausage in the identical way and cook until heated through, about 3 minutes. Add sausage into patty pan mix.

❖ Fold in goat milk, Parmesan cheese, and tomato. Add hot sauce and season with pepper and salt. Twist in patty pan-sausage mix. Put frittata mixture to the prepared muffin cups, filling to the peak of every cup and then overfilling only when the parchment paper may encourage the mix.

❖ Put muffin tin in addition to a cookie sheet in the middle of the toaster.

8. **Bacon and Cheese Frittata**

Ingredients

- ½ cup cheddar cheese, grated

- 4 eggs

- ½ cup chopped, cooked bacon

- ½ tsp salt

- 3 Tbsp. heavy whipping cream

- ¼ tsp ground black pepper

Method:

❖ Preheat your air fryer to 350 degrees F and line a baking pan using parchment paper. Be sure the pan will fit on your fryer- normally a seven inch round pan will do the job flawlessly.

❖ In a small bowl, whisk together the eggs, cream, pepper and salt

❖ Stir in the cheese and bacon into the bowl.

❖ Pour the mixture into the prepared baking pan then place the pan on your preheated air fryer.

❖ Cook for approximately 15 minutes or till the eggs are completely set.

9. Meat Lovers Omelet

Ingredients:

● ¼ cup cheddar cheese, grated

● ¼ cup cooked, crumbled bacon

● ½ tsp salt

● 4 eggs

● ¼ cup cooked, crumbled sausage

● 3 Tbsp. heavy whipping cream

● ¼ tsp ground black pepper

Method:

❑ Preheat your air fryer to 350 degrees F and line a baking pan using parchment paper. Be sure the pan will fit on your fryer- normally a seven inch round pan will do the job flawlessly.

❏ In a small bowl whisk together the eggs, cream, pepper and salt.

❏ Pour the mixture into the prepared baking pan then place the pan on your preheated air fryer.

❏ Cook for approximately ten minutes or till the eggs are completely set.

❏ Sprinkle the cheeses round the boiled eggs and then return the pan into the fryer for another two minutes to melt the cheese.

10. Crispy Brussels sprouts

Next on our list is air fryer crispy Brussels sprouts.

Ingredients:

- Brussels sprouts

- Salt

- Pepper

Method:

Let's get started with these Brussels sprouts. Use fresh Brussels sprouts and we could also use frozen ones. I've got a bag of frozen Brussels sprouts and actually they're still broke. I'm going to season them with some salt and some pepper.

Shake them up and now I'm going to cook them at 400 or I'm going to start with 10 minutes. Let's see how it goes. I think you're going to be surprised because they're crispy. Can you believe that? I think these are better than fresh ones.

Use frozen if you want to make air fryer Brussels sprouts because the fresh ones take forever to get soft on the inside. You got to cut them into quarters, you've got to trim the leaves off these. They're frozen. I just threw them in the air fryer for 15minutes and they're good to go.

Now what I'm going to show you are actually dessert ideas that you can cook in your air fryer. They come in different sizes and one and a half liter is quite common too, so just check when you buy your own if you do that.

It is a bigger liter air fryer because I promise you, you're going to want to cook everything in this. What I love about this style of air fryer is that it's so simple on the front. You will see that you have got different settings but if you want to cook chips, prawns, fish, steak and muffins as well, it's really easy to adjust the temperature up and down. Also the time up and down as well. Then once you put your tray back in, all you need to do is select your setting and press the play button and the air fryer does everything else for you. It is also really really easy to clean. All you need to do is remove your tray from your air fryer, press the button on at the handle and detach your basket from the tray.

I then use a handheld scrubbing brush which dispenses washing-up liquid and I just go over my basket and my outer tray as well which is where all the fats from your food drip. I just go in with some warm water and my washing up liquid washes it all away. It's got a really nice TEFL coating so everything just wipes off. It's nonstick, then I just leave it on the side, let it dry and then pop it back in my air fryer. At once it is dry, so with all that said I'm just going to jump straight on into the recipes.

11. Hard Boiled Eggs

Ingredients:

- 4 eggs

Method:

➢ Preheat your air fryer to 250 degrees F.

➢ Place a wire rack in the fryer and set the eggs in addition to the rack.

➢ Cook for 17 minutes then remove the eggs and put them into an

➢ Ice water bath to cool and then stop the cooking procedure.

➢ Peel the eggs and love!

1. Spinach Parmesan Baked Eggs

Ingredients:

- 1 Tbsp. frozen, chopped spinach, thawed

- 1 Tbsp. grated parmesan cheese

- 2 eggs

- 1 Tbsp. heavy cream

- ¼ tsp salt

- 1/8 tsp ground black pepper

Method:

❏ Preheat your air fryer to 330 degrees F.

❏ Spray a silicone muffin cup or a little ramekin with cooking spray.

❏ In a small bowl, whisk together all of the components

❏ Pour the eggs into the ready ramekin and bake for 2 minutes.

❏ Enjoy directly from the skillet!

12.Fried hushpuppies.

Inside my home, stuffing is consistently the very popular Thanksgiving dish on the table. Because of this, we create double the amount we all actually need just so we can eat leftovers for a week! And while remaining stuffing alone is yummy, turning it into hushpuppies? Now that is only pure wizardry. Here is the way to use your air fryer to produce near-instant two-ingredient fried hushpuppies.

Ingredients:

- large egg

- cold stuffing

- Cooking spray

Directions:

★ Put 1 large egg in a large bowl and gently beat. Add 3 cups leftover stuffing and stir till blended.

★ Preheat in an air fryer into 355ºF and place it for 12 minutes. Put one layer of hushpuppies on the racks and then spray the tops with cooking spray.

★ Repeat with the remaining mixture.

13.Keto Breakfast Pizza

An egg, sausage, and pork rind "crust" holds sauce, cheese, and other savory toppings within this keto-friendly breakfast pizza recipe.

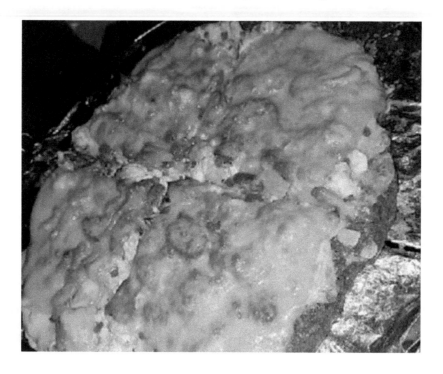

Ingredients

- 3 large eggs, split

- 2 tbsp. Italian seasoning

- 1 cup ready country-style sauce

- 10 tbsp. bacon pieces

- 1 pound bulk breakfast sausage

- cooking spray

- 1/3 cup crushed pork rinds

- 2 tbsp. chopped yellow onion

- 2 tbsp. diced jalapeno pepper

- 1 cup shredded Cheddar cheese

Instructions

★ Grease a rimmed pizza sheet.

★ Spread mixture out on the pizza sheet at a big, thin circle.

★ Meanwhile, spray a large air fryer with cooking spray and heat over medium-high heat. Whisk remaining eggs together in a bowl and then pour into it.

★ Place an oven rack about 6 inches from the heat source and then turn on the oven's broiler.

★ Spread sausage evenly over the beef "crust", sprinkle scrambled eggs. Sprinkle with bacon pieces, onion, and jalapeno.

★ Broil pizza in the preheated oven till cheese is melted, bubbling, and lightly browned, 3 to 5 minutes. Let cool and cut into fourths prior to serving.

14. Mozzarella stick

Ready for the simplest mozzarella stick recipe? These air fryer mozzarella sticks are created completely from pantry and refrigerator staples (cheese sticks and breadcrumbs), which means that you can dig to the crispy-coated, nostalgic bite anytime you would like.

INGREDIENTS:

- ➢ 1 (12-ounce) bundle mayonnaise
- ➢ 1 large egg
- ➢ 1/2 tsp garlic powder
- ➢ all-purpose flour
- ➢ 1/2 tsp onion powder

Method:

★ Before frying pan, set the halved cheese sticks onto a rimmed baking sheet lined with parchment paper. Freeze for half an hour. Meanwhile, construct the breading and get outside the air fryer.

★ Whisk the egg and lettuce together in a skillet. Put the flour, breadcrumbs, onion, and garlic powder in a large bowl and whisk to mix.

★ Working in batches of 6, then roll the suspended cheese sticks at the mayo-egg mix to coat, and then in the flour mixture.

★ Pour the coated cheese sticks into the parchment-lined baking sheet. Pour the baking sheet into the freezer for 10 minutes.

★ Heat the fryer to 370°F. Fry 6 the mozzarella sticks for 5 minutes -- it's important not to overcrowd the fryer.

★ Repeat with the rest of the sticks and serve hot with the marinara for dipping.

15. Raspberry Muffins

Ingredients:

- ¼ cup whole milk

- 1 egg

- 1 Tbsp. powdered stevia

- ¼ tsp salt

- ¼ tsp ground cinnamon

- 1 ½ tsp baking powder

- 1 cup almond flour

- ½ cup frozen or fresh raspberries

Steps:

I.   Preheat your air fryer to 350 degrees F.

II. In a large bowl, stir together the almond milk, stevia, salt, cinnamon, and baking powder.

III. Add the milk and eggs and then stir well.

IV. Split the muffin batter involving each muffin cup, filling roughly 3/4 of this way complete.

V.   Set the muffins to the fryer basket and cook for 14 minutes or till a toothpick comes out when inserted to the middle.

VI.   Eliminate from the fryer and let cool.

16. Sausage Tray Bake

I have just chopped up some new potatoes and then I've got some chipolata sausages so I'm going to make a tray bake.

Ingredients:

- Potatoes

- Chipolata Sausage

- corvette

- Onion

- Garlic

Method:

I would put potato and chipotle sausage into the air fryer for about 20 minutes at first before I add in my other veggies.

Once these have been in for 20 minutes or so, I will then add in two papers of corvette, an onion and some garlic to go in as well. Cook them for a further 10 minutes and then dinner should be ready.

17.Strawberry Muffins

Ingredients:

- ¼ cup whole milk

- 1 ½ tsp baking powder

- ½ cup chopped strawberries

- 1 egg

- ¼ tsp salt

- ¼ tsp ground cinnamon

- 1 cup almond flour

- 1 Tbsp. powdered stevia

Steps:

1.   Preheat your air fryer to 350 degrees F.

2. In a large bowl, stir together the almond milk, stevia, salt, cinnamon, and baking powder.

3. Add the milk and eggs and then stir well.

4. Fold in the berries.

5. Split the muffin batter involving each muffin cup, filling roughly 3/4 of this way complete.

6. Set the muffins to the fryer basket and cook for 14 minutes or till a toothpick comes out when inserted to the middle.

7. Eliminate from the fryer and let cool.

18. Bacon and Eggs for a single

Ingredients:

- 1 Tbsp. heavy cream

- two Tbsp. cooked, crumbled bacon

- 1/4 tsp salt

- 2 eggs

- 1/8 tsp ground black pepper

Directions

❏ Preheat your air fryer to 330 degrees F.

❏ Spray a silicone muffin cup or a little ramekin with cooking spray.

❏ In a small bowl, whisk together all of the components

❏ Pour the eggs into the ready ramekin and bake for 2 minutes.

❏ Enjoy directly from the skillet!

19. Mini Sausage Pancake Skewers with Spicy Syrup

These small savory skewers are fantastic for breakfast or a fantastic addition to your brunch buffet. The hot maple syrup garnish kicks up the flavor and adds some zest to sandwiches and sausage.

Ingredients

Syrup:

- 4 tbsp. unsalted butter

- 1/2 tsp salt

- 1/2 cup maple syrup

- 1 tsp red pepper flakes, or to taste

Pancake

- 1 cup buttermilk

- 2 tbsp. unsalted butter, melted

- 1 cup all-purpose flour

- 1 large egg

- 1 tbsp. olive oil

- 1 lb. ounce standard pork sausage (like Jimmy Dean®)

- 13 4-inch bamboo skewers

- 2 tablespoons sour cream

- 1/2 tbsp. brown sugar

- 1/4 tsp baking powder

- 1/4 tsp salt

- 2 tsp maple syrup

Instructions

- ❏ Bring to a boil and cook for 3 to 4 minutes.

❏ Meanwhile, prepare pancakes: whisk flour, sugar, baking powder, and salt in a huge bowl. Whisk buttermilk, egg, sour cream, melted butter and maple syrup together in another bowl. Pour the wet ingredients into the flour mixture. Stir lightly until just blended but slightly lumpy; don't overmix. Let sit for 10 minutes.

❏ Heat in an air fryer over moderate heat. Drop teaspoonfuls of batter onto them to make 1-inch diameter sandwiches.

❏ Cook for approximately 1 to 2 minutes, then reverse, and keep cooking until golden brown, about 1 minute. Transfer cooked pancakes into a plate and repeat with remaining batter.

❏ Heat olive oil at precisely the exact same fryer over moderate heat. Form table-spoonfuls of sausage to 1-inch patties, exactly the exact same size as the miniature pancakes.

❏ Cook until patties are cooked through, about 3 minutes each side. Transfer to a newspaper towel-lined plate.

❏ Blend 3 pancakes and two sausage patties onto each skewer, beginning and end with a pancake.

❏ Repeat to create staying skewers. Serve drizzled with hot syrup.

20. Avocado Baked Eggs

Ingredients:

- 1 Tbsp. heavy cream

- ¼ tsp salt

- ¼ avocado, diced

- 1 Tbsp. grated cheddar cheese

- 2 eggs

- 1/8 tsp ground black pepper

Method:

❏ Preheat your air fryer to 330 degrees F.

❏ Spray a silicone muffin cup or a little ramekin with cooking spray.

❏ In a small bowl, whisk together the eggs, cream, cheddar cheese, salt, and pepper.

❏ Stir in the avocado and pour the eggs into the ready ramekin and bake for 2 minutes.

❏ Enjoy directly from the skillet!

Chapter 2: Air Fryer 50 more Recipes for You!

21. Sausage and Cheese Omelet

Ingredients:

- ¼ cup cheddar cheese, grated

- ½ cup cooked, crumbled sausage

- 4 eggs

- 3 Tbsp. heavy whipping cream

- ½ tsp salt

- ¼ tsp ground black pepper

Method

01. Preheat your air fryer to 320 degrees F and line a baking pan using parchment paper. Be sure the pan will fit on your fryer- normally a seven inch round pan will do the job flawlessly.

02. In a small bowl, whisk together the eggs, cream, pepper and salt.

03. Pour the mixture into the prepared baking pan then place the pan on your preheated air fryer.

04. Cook for approximately ten minutes or till the eggs are completely set.

05. Sprinkle the cheeses round the boiled eggs and then return the pan into the fryer for another two minutes to melt the cheese.

22. Pita bread Pizza

I am making some pita bread pizzas now.

Ingredients:

- Bread

- Tomato puree

- Passat

Method:

I usually would make these in the oven and I would put them in there for about 10 to 15 minutes. I'm just going to put some ketchup on top of the pizza bread base.

Or you can put tomato puree on there or some pasta whatever you've got. Then I'm just going to put some cheese on really nice and simple. I'm going to pop them on the pizza setting in the air fryer so that's eight minutes when I do my pizzas in the oven the base isn't really nice and crispy. So, I am really pleased with how they've turned out in the air fryer. Pizzas are done, crispy delicious, ready to eat.

23. Air Fryer Hanukkah Latkes

If you have never needed a latke, it is about time we change this. Traditionally served throughout Hanukkah, these crispy fritters -- frequently made with grated potatoes, lettuce, onion, and matzo meal -- are kind of impossible to not love.

Traditionally latkes are fried in oil (or poultry schmaltz!)) , however I wanted to see if I could create them using the popular air fryer. Since the fryer is a high-heat convection oven, the large fan speed and focused warmth yields a crispy potato pancake that is also soft at the middle.

INGREDIENTS

- 1 1/2 Pounds Russet potatoes (2 to 3 tbsp.)

- ½ medium yellow onion

- 1/2 tsp freshly ground black pepper

- Cooking spray

- Two large eggs

- matzo meal

- 2 tsp kosher salt

Description:

❖ Peel 1 1/2 lbs. russet potatoes. Grate the potatoes and 1/2 yellow onion onto the large holes of a box grater. Put with a clean kitchen towel, then pull up the sides of the towel to make a package, and squeeze out excess moisture.

❖ Transfer the curry mixture into a large bowl. Add two large eggs, 1/4 cup matzo meal, two tsp kosher salt, and 1/2 tsp black pepper, and stir to blend.

❖ Preheat the Air Fryer into 375ºF and place it for 16 minutes. Coat the air fryer racks together with cooking spray.

❖ Dip the latke mix in 2-tablespoon dollops to the fryer, flattening the shirts to make a patty.

❖ Air fry, rotating the trays halfway through, for 2 minutes total. Repeat with the rest of the latke mix.

24. Salmon Fillet

Now, I'm going to cook some salmon in it.

Ingredients:

- Salmon

Method:

I put my salmon in, with nothing on top of it, just a salmon filet. I pop it in on the fish sitting for ten minutes and when it comes out it has got the crispy skin ever. The salmon was in for ten minutes and I wanted to show you how crispy the skin is.

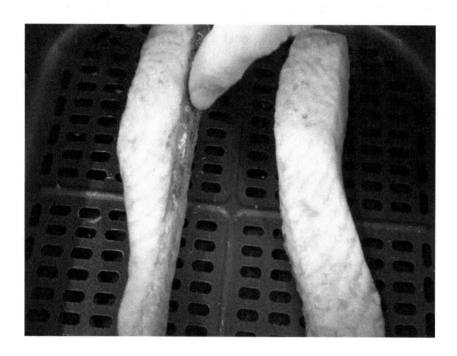

I'm someone who loves eating salmon skin and that is just perfectly done right.

25. Air Fryer Mini Calzones

Among the greatest approaches to utilize an air fryer is a miniature oven that will not heat up your entire kitchen for party snacks. It's possible to turn out batch after batch of wings, mozzarella sticks, and also, yes, miniature calzones which are hot, crispy, and superbly nostalgic by one air fryer.

These mini calzones utilize ready pizza dough to produce delicious pockets full of gooey cheese, piquant tomato sauce, and hot pepperoni that are fantastic for celebrations, after-school snacks, or even for satisfying your craving to get your dessert rolls of your childhood.

Ingredients:

- All-purpose flour, for rolling the dough out

- Pizza sauce, and more for dipping

- Thinly sliced pepperoni

- miniature pepperoni, chopped

Directions:

- ❖ Utilize a 3-inch round cutter or a large glass to cut 8 to 10 rounds of bread.

- ❖ Transfer the rounds into some parchment paper-lined baking sheet. Gather up the dough scraps, then reroll and replicate cutting rounds out until you've got 16.

- ❖ Top each round with two tsp of sauce, 1 tablespoon of cheese, and one tsp of pepperoni.

- ❖ Working with a single dough around at a time, fold in half an hour, then pinch the edges together to seal. When every calzone is sealed, then use a fork to crimp the borders shut to additional seal.

❖ Heat the air fryer into 375°F. Working in batches of 4, air fry the calzones until golden brown and crispy, about 8 minutes. Serve with extra pizza sauce for dipping, if desired.

26. Fajitas

Ingredients:

- Turkey Strips

- Yellow Pepper

- Onion

- Orange Pepper

Method:

It's a night that we are going to be having for heaters. So, here, I've chopped up yellow and orange pepper and also half an onion. I have got some turkey strips.

I'll pass it over heat as it makes barbecue flavor onto all of this. So, I'm just going to pop these all into the air fryer together because I think they'll actually cook through at a very similar rate. Then I am going to pop them on the chicken setting and let the air fryer get cooking alright. This is the fajita mix in ten minutes.

I put on the chicken setting which is actually 20 minutes but I was just checking it.

I cut a piece of the turkey and it's perfect all the way through, I cut it like one of the biggest pieces up as well. So, it's absolutely perfect so all this needs is ten minutes in the air fryer and it's done right.

27.Pot Sweet Potato Chips

Replace the humble sweet potato to a freshly-fried bite, and it is sure to be yummy. Sweet potato chips, sweet potato tater tots -- you name it, we will take it.

The comparison between the sweetness of the curry and the saltiness of this bite is really impossible to not love.

These air fryer sweet potato chips provide everything you adore about these deep-fried snacks. That is the great thing about the air fryer that it requires less oil, after all -- you have to bypass the hassle and clutter of heating a massive pot of oil to the stove -- but the "fried" cure comes out evenly as yummy. And unlike a store-bought bag of chips, you have to personalize the seasonings. Here, we are using dried herbs and a pinch of cayenne for an earthy, somewhat spicy beverage.

Ingredients:

- medium sweet potato

- 1 tbsp. canola oil

- 1/2 tsp freshly ground black pepper

- 1/4 tsp paprika

- 1 tsp kosher salt

- 3/4 tsp dried thyme leaves

- Cooking spray

Directions:

❏ Wash 1 sweet potato and dry nicely. Thinly slice 1/8-inch thick using a knife or rather on a mandolin. Set in a bowl, then cover with cool water, and then soak at room temperature for 20 minutes to remove the excess starch.

❏ Drain the pieces and pat very dry with towels. Put into a large bowl, then add 1 tbsp. canola oil, 1 tsp kosher salt, 3/4 tsp dried thyme leaves, 1/2 tsp black pepper, 1/4 tsp paprika, and a pinch cayenne pepper if using, and toss to blend.

❏ Gently coat in an air fryer rotisserie basket with cooking spray.

❏ Air fry in batches: put one layer of sweet potato pieces from the rotisserie basket. Put the rotisserie basket at the fryer and press on.

❏ Preheat the fryer into 340°F and place for 22 minutes, until the sweet potatoes are golden brown and the edges are crispy, 19 to 22 minutes.

❏ Transfer the chips into a newspaper towel-lined plate to cool completely

❏ They will crisp as they cool. Repeat with the remaining sweet potato pieces.

28. Easy Baked Eggs

Ingredients:

- 1 Tbsp. heavy cream

- ¼ tsp salt

- 2 eggs

- 1/8 tsp ground black pepper

Method:

➢ Preheat your fryer to 330 degrees F.

➢ Spray a silicone muffin cup or a little ramekin with cooking spray.

➢ In a small bowl, whisk together all of the components

➢ Pour the eggs into the ready ramekin and bake for 6 minutes.

➢ Enjoy directly from the skillet!

29. Air Fryer Buttermilk Fried Chicken

I went to school in the South, so I have had my fair share of crispy, succulent, finger-licking fried chicken. As you might imagine, I had been skeptical about creating a much healthier version from the air fryer.

The second I pulled out my first batch, but my worries disappeared. The epidermis was crispy, the coat was cracker-crisp (as it ought to be), and also, above all, the chicken itself was tender and succulent -- the indication of a perfect piece of fried chicken.

Air fryer fried chicken is lighter, quicker, than and not as cluttered as deep-fried chicken. Here is the way to get it done.

Ingredients

- 1 tsp Freshly ground black pepper, divided

- Buttermilk

- 1 tsp Cayenne pepper

- 1 tbsp. Garlic powder

- 2 tbsp. paprika

- 1 tbsp. onion powder

- 1 tsp kosher salt, divided

- all-purpose flour

- 1 tbsp. ground mustard

- Cooking spray

Directions

- ❏ Put all ingredients into a large bowl and season with 1 teaspoon of the kosher salt and 1/2 tsp of honey.

- ❏ Add 2 cups buttermilk and simmer for 1 hour in the fridge. Meanwhile, whisk the remaining 1 tbsp. kosher salt, staying 1/2 tsp black pepper, 2 cups all-purpose flour, 1 tbsp. garlic powder, 2 tbsp. paprika, 1 teaspoon cayenne pepper, 1 tbsp. onion powder, plus one tbsp. ground mustard together into a huge bowl.

❑ Preheat an air fryer into 390°F. Coat the fryer racks together with cooking spray. Remove the chicken in the buttermilk, allowing any excess to drip off. Dredge in the flour mixture, shaking off any excess. Put one layer of chicken in the basket, with distance between the bits. Air fry, turning the chicken hallway through, until an instant-read thermometer registers 165°F from the thickest part

❑ Cook for 18 to 20 minutes, then complete.

30. Keto Chocolate Chip Muffins

Ingredients:

- ¼ tsp salt

- 1 Tbsp. powdered stevia

- ¼ cup whole milk

- 1 egg

- 1 cup almond flour

- 1 ½ tsp baking powder

- ½ cup mini dark chocolate chips (sugar free)

Method:

❖ Preheat your air fryer to 350 degrees F.

❖ In a large bowl, stir together the almond milk, stevia, salt, cinnamon, and baking powder.

❖ Add the milk and eggs and then stir well.

❖ Split the muffin batter involving each muffin cup, filling around 3/4 of this way complete.

❖ Set the muffins to the air fryer basket and cook for 14 minutes or till a toothpick comes out when put to the middle.

❖ Eliminate from the fryer and let cool.

31. Crispy Chickpeas

What, I've got in here are some chickpeas.

Ingredients:

- Chickpeas

- Olive oil

- Per-peril salt

Method:

I've drained and washed chickpeas and then what I'm going to do is add on some olive oil and then also the periphery salt. The reason I put some olive oil on is because it just helps the pair of results stick to the chickpeas.

Then I'm just going to mix everything in together and pop them into the air fryer for about 15 minutes. On the chip setting these are great little snacks to make like pre dinner snacks. Instead of having crisps or if you're watching a movie, instead of having popcorn these are good little things. Also, if you are having a salad they're really nice to go in your salad as well.

32. Keto Blueberry Muffins

Ingredients:

- 1 egg

- ¼ tsp salt

- 1 cup almond flour

- 1 Tbsp. powdered stevia

- 1 ½ tsp baking powder

- ¼ cup whole milk

- ¼ tsp ground cinnamon

- ½ cup frozen or fresh blueberries

Steps:

1) Preheat your air fryer to 350 degrees F.

2) In a large bowl, stir together the almond milk, stevia, salt, cinnamon, and baking powder.

3) Add the milk and eggs and then stir well.

4) Split the muffin batter involving each muffin cup, filling roughly 3/4 of this way complete.

5) Set the muffins to the air fryer basket and cook for 14 minutes or till a toothpick comes out when put to the middle.

6) Eliminate from the fryer and let cool.

33.Air Fryer Donuts

Ingredients

- ground cinnamon

- granulated sugar

- Flaky large snacks,

- Jojoba oil spray or coconut oil spray

Instructions

★ Combine sugar and cinnamon in a shallow bowl; place aside.

★ Remove the cookies from the tin, separate them and set them onto the baking sheet.

★ Utilize a 1-inch round biscuit cutter (or similarly-sized jar cap) to cut holes from the middle of each biscuit.

★ Lightly coat an air fryer basket using coconut or olive oil spray (don't use nonstick cooking spray like Pam, which may damage the coating onto the basket)

★ Put 3 to 4 donuts in one layer in the air fryer (that they shouldn't be touching). Close to the air fryer and place to 350°F. Transfer donuts into the baking sheet.

★ Repeat with the rest of the biscuits. You can also cook the donut holes they will take approximately 3 minutes total

★ Brush both sides of this hot donut with melted butter, put in the cinnamon sugar, and then turn to coat both sides.

34. Sausage and Spinach Omelet

Ingredients:

½ cup baby spinach

4 eggs

¼ cup cheddar cheese, grated

½ cup cooked, crumbled sausage

3 Tbsp. heavy whipping cream

½ tsp salt

¼ tsp ground black pepper

Directions

I.   Preheat the air fryer at around 330 F.

II.   In a small bowl, whisk together the eggs, cream, pepper and salt.

III. Fold in the cooked sausage and sausage.

IV.   Pour the mixture into the prepared baking pan then place the pan on your

V.   Cook for approximately ten minutes or till the eggs are completely set.

VI.   Sprinkle the cheeses round the boiled eggs and then return the pan into the fryer

VII. Fryer for another two minutes to melt the cheese.

35. **Air Fryer Potato Wedges**

Perfectly crisp and seasoned potato wedges directly from your air fryer. It will not get any simpler than this!

Ingredients

→ 2 medium Russet potatoes, cut into wedges

→ 1/2 tsp sea salt

→ 1 1/2 tsp olive oil

→ 1/2 tsp chili powder

→ ⅛ teaspoon ground black pepper

→ 1/2 tsp paprika

→ 1/2 tsp parsley flakes

Instructions

❖ Place potato wedges in a large bowl.

❖ Put 8 wedges at the jar of the air fryer and cook for 10 minutes.

❖ Flip wedges with tongs and cook for another five minutes.

36. Chocolate Chip Cookies in Air fryer

They are my day pick-me-up, my after-dinner treat, also, sometimes, a part of my breakfast. I keep either frozen cookies or baked biscuits in my freezer -- true my friends know and have come to appreciate when they come around for dinner or even a glass of wine.

The kind of chocolate chip cookie I enjoy all, depends upon my mood. Sometimes I need them super doughy, and sometimes challenging and crisp. If you're searching for one someplace in between -- gooey on the inside and crunchy on the outside -- I have discovered the foolproof way of you. It entails cooking them on your air fryer.

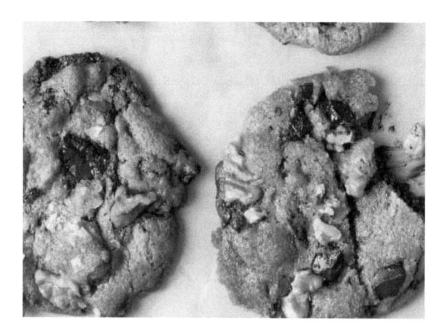

When using your fryer to create biscuits, be certain that you always line its base with foil to aid with simple cleanup. You will also need to line the basket or racks using parchment paper. Buy paper which has holes in it, cut some slits to the newspaper, or make sure you leave space around it which will allow for even cooking and flow of the air. With these suggestions, you're on your way to cookie victory!

Ingredients:

- Granulated sugar

- vanilla extract

- dark brown sugar

- 1 tsp kosher salt

- 2 large eggs

- 3/4 cup chopped walnuts

- 1 tsp baking soda

- Flaky sea salt, for garnish (optional)

- all-purpose flour

- Cooking spray

INSTRUCTIONS

❖ Put 2 sticks unsalted butter in the bowl of a stand mixer, fitted with the paddle attachment and also let it sit till softened. Insert 3/4 cup granulated sugar and 3/4 cup packed dark brown sugar and beat it on medium speed till blended and fluffy within 3 to 4 minutes. Add 1 tablespoon lemon extract, 2 big eggs, and 1 tsp kosher salt, and beat until just blended. After that, add 1 tea-spoon baking soda plus 2 1/3 cups all-purpose flour in increments, mixing until just blended.

❖ Add 2 cups chocolate balls and 3/4 cup chopped peppers and stir with a rubber spatula until just blended.

❖ Preheat in an air fryer, at 350°F and set to 5 minutes. Line the fryer racks with parchment paper, make sure you leave space on all sides for air to leak.

❖ Reduce 2-tablespoon scoops of this dough on the racks, setting them 1-inch apart. Gently flatten each spade marginally to earn a cookie form.

❖ Sprinkle with flaky sea salt, if using. Bake until golden brown, about 5 minutes. Remove the racks out of the fryer and let it cool for 3 to 5 minutes to place. Repeat with the remaining dough.

37.Crispy Coated Veggies

Ingredients:

- Vegetables

- Egg

- Paprika

- Salt & Pepper

Method:

I'm making some crispy coating of vegetables in this bowl. I have got one egg beaten up. This is actually almond flour but you can use normal flour and then I popped in some paprika. I've also put in some salt and pepper here too. Then I'm going to dip my veggies into my egg and then I'll put them into the flour mixture, then into the air fryer for probably about eight minutes.

38. Ranch Pork Chops in Air fryer

Ingredients

- 4 boneless, center-cut pork chops, 1-inch thick

- aluminum foil

- cooking spray

- 2 Tsp dry ranch salad dressing mix

Directions

★ Put pork chops on a plate and then gently spray both sides with cooking spray. Sprinkle both sides with ranch seasoning mixture and let them sit at room temperature for 10 minutes.

★ Spray the basket of an air fryer with cooking spray and preheat at 390 degrees F (200 degrees C).

★ Place chops in the preheated air fryer, working in batches if needed, to guarantee the fryer isn't overcrowded.

★ Flip chops and cook for 5 minutes longer. Let rest on a foil-covered plate for 5 minutes prior to serving.

39. Quesadillas

Ingredients:

- Refried Beans

- Cheese

- Peppers

- Chicken

Method:

I'm going to be using the El Paso refried beans in the tin. I will spread that onto the wrap and then I'm just going to sprinkle some cheese on top.

This is a really basic wrap so usually when we have routes we'll add some like peppers in here as well and loads of other bits like chicken. I just wanted to show you how well they cook in the air fryer. You pop them in on the pizza setting and in 8 to10 minutes they are done. Really crispy and ready to eat.

40. Pecan Crusted Pork Chops at the Air Fryer

The air-fryer makes simple work of those yummy pork chops. The chops make good leftovers too, since the pecan crust does not get soggy!

Ingredients:

- Egg

- Pork

- Pecans

- Simmer

Instructions

➤ Add egg and simmer until all ingredients are well blended. Place pecans onto a plate.

➤ Dip each pork dip in the egg mix, then put onto the plate together with the pecans

➤ Press pecans firmly onto either side until coated. Spray the chops on both sides with cooking spray and set from the fryer basket.

➤ Cook at the fryer for 6 minutes. Turn chops closely with tongs, and fry until pork is no longer pink in the middle, about 6 minutes more.

41. Crispy Chicken Thighs

Ingredients

- Chicken thighs

- Pepper

- Olive oil

- Paprika

- Salt

Method:

I've got some chicken thighs. These have got bone-in and skinned on so what I've done is just put some olive oil on top of them with some paprika and some salt and pepper. Then I just rubbed everything into the chicken skin so I'm going to pop these into my air fryer. Press the chicken button and let the air fryer just do its thing.

This skin is super crispy that is perfectly done and it's been in there for 20 minutes. I just wanted to show you all the fat that came out of that chicken so here are all the oils that came off.

So those are what your chicken would be sitting in but instead it's all just tripped underneath the air fryer.

42. Bacon-Wrapped Scallops with Sirach Mayo

This yummy appetizer is ready quickly and easily in the air fryer and served with a hot Sirach mayo skillet. I use the smaller bay scallops because of this. If you're using jumbo scallops, it'll require a longer cooking time and more bits of bacon.

Ingredients

- 1/2 cup mayonnaise

- 1 pinch coarse salt

- 2 tbsp. Sirach sauce

- 1 pound bay scallops (about 36 small scallops)

- 1 pinch freshly cracked black pepper

- 12 slices bacon, cut into thirds

- 1 serving olive oil cooking spray

Instructions

★ Mix mayonnaise and Sirach sauce together in a little bowl.

★ Preheat the air fryer to 390 degrees F (200 degrees C).

★ Season with pepper and salt. Wrap each scallop with 1/3 piece of bacon and fasten with a toothpick.

★ Spray the air fryer basket with cooking spray. Put bacon-wrapped scallops from the basket in one layer; divide into two batches if needed.

★ Cook at the air fryer for 7 minutes. Check for doneness; scallops should be wheat and opaque ought to be crispy. Cook 1 to 2 minutes more, if needed, checking every moment. Remove scallops carefully with tongs and put on a newspaper towel-lined plate to absorb extra oil out of the bacon.

43.Homemade Chips

Ingredients

- Chip

- Olive oil

- Paprika

- Salt

Method:

Now I'm going to do some chips. I've just cut up some potatoes into chip shapes and then I am going to put some olive oil on top. Some paprika and some salt and the main reason I'm putting olive oil on top is basically for the paprika and the salt to stick to the surface of the chips. I'll just pop these in and then I'll put them onto the chip setting and let them cook away for about 18 minutes. I will be staring these halfway through because I'm doing quite a few chips as well. I will probably have to put these on for another 10 minutes after the 18 minutes is done.

44. Easy Air Fryer Pork Chops

Boneless pork chops cooked to perfection with the help of an air fryer. This recipe is super easy and you could not ask for a more tender and succulent chop.

Ingredients

- 1/2 cup grated Parmesan cheese

- 1 tsp kosher salt

- 4 (5 oz.) center-cut pork chops

- 2 tbsp. extra virgin olive oil

- 1 tsp dried parsley

- 1 tsp paprika

- 1 tsp garlic powder

- 1/2 teaspoon ground black pepper

Instructions

❑ Preheat the fryer to 390 degrees F.

❑ Combine Parmesan cheese, paprika, garlic powder, salt, parsley, and pepper in a level shallow dish; combine well.

❑ Stir every pork chop with olive oil. Dredge both sides of each dip from the Parmesan mixture and put on a plate.

❑ Put 2 chops from the basket of the fryer and cook for 10 minutes; turning halfway through cook time.

45. Corn on the Cob

Ingredients:

- Corn

- Butter

- Salt

Method:

We're going to do some corn on the cob. What I'm going to do is just pop them into my air fryer but not put anything on top of them. I'm going to put them in on the prawn settings.

It's just eight minutes, after ten minutes like I said, I will then add some butter on top and a little bit of salt. They're ready to eat.

46. Air Fryer Broiled Grapefruit

This hot and warm grapefruit with a buttery candy topping is the best accompaniment for your Sunday brunch and makes a lovely snack or dessert. I love to add a pinch of sea salt in the end to actually bring out the tastes.

Ingredients

- 1 red grapefruit, refrigerated

- aluminum foil

- 1 tbsp. brown sugar

- 1/2 teaspoon ground cinnamon

- 1 tbsp. softened butter

- 2 tsp sugar

Instructions

➢ Cut grapefruit in half crosswise and slice off a thin sliver away from the base of every half, when the fruit is not sitting at level. Use a sharp paring knife to cut around the outer edge of this grapefruit and involve every section to generate the fruit easier to consume after cooking.

➢ Combine softened butter 1 tbsp. brown sugar in a small bowl. Spread mix over each grapefruit in half. Sprinkle with remaining brown sugar levels.

➢ Cut aluminum foil into two 5-inch squares and put each grapefruit half one square; fold the edges up to catch any juices. Place in the air fryer basket.

➢ Broil in the fryer until the sugar mixture is bubbling, 6 to 7 minutes.

47.Kale Crisps

Ingredients:

- Kale

- Olive oil

- Salt

Method:

I'm going to make some kale crisps now. So, the first thing we're going to do list, get my kale and chop off the thick stocky bits. Once I've chopped that out, I will then just dice my kale up into kind of chunks and then I'll pop them into a bowl. Put some olive oil on top and some salts give everything a mix around.

I'll pop them into my air fryer and on the prong setting. The reason I put them on the prong setting is because that's just a quick eight minute setting and that's the perfect amount of time that these kale crisps take to cook. When they come out, they are super nice and crunchy and they taste delicious.

48. Air Fryer Brown Sugar and Pecan Roasted Apples

A sweet and nutty topping made with brown sugar and pecans adds amazing flavor to apples since they cook to tender perfection at the air fryer.

Ingredients

- 1/4 tsp apple pie spice

- 2 tbsp. coarsely chopped pecans

- 1 tbsp. brown sugar

- 1 tbsp. butter, melted

- 1 tsp all-purpose flour

- 2 medium apples, cored and cut into wedges

Instructions

→ Preheat the air fryer to 350 degrees F

→ Put apple wedges in a skillet drizzle with butter and toss to coat. Arrange apples in one layer in the air fryer basket and then sprinkle with pecan mixture.

→ Cook in the preheated air fryer until apples are tender, 10 to 15 minutes.

49.Sausage Rolls

Ingredients:

- Sausage

- Puff pastry

- Cheese

- Chutney

- Milk

Methods:

Today we're going to make some really easy sausage rolls. So, I've just got some puff pastry and some sausages. What I'll do is I'll cut the puff pastry into four pieces. I'll then lay a sausage into each one of the pieces along with some grated cheese.

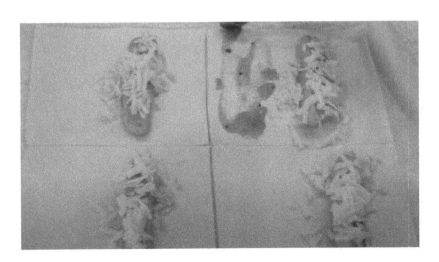

I like to have some chutney in the house as well. I'll just fold over the pastry and then secure it with a fork at the edges. So, it doesn't open up. I then just also get a bit of milk as well or you can use a beaten egg and just brush it over the top so it goes nice and golden brown. I'll pop it into my air fryer on the chip setting because they do need a good18 minutes in there to make sure the sausages are nice and cooked.

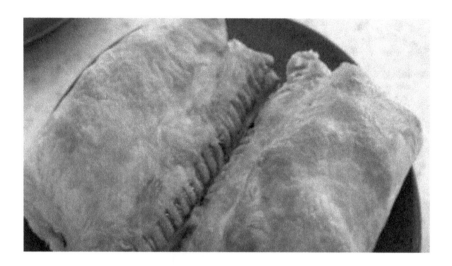

After the 18 minutes they're ready to eat.

50. Air Fryer French Fries

It will not get more classic than French fries; the normally accepted technique is fairly, dare I say, air tight, but I really do have one additional trick in shop! Last, dip them in honey mustard, hot ketchup, garlic aioli, or all 3 blended together, such as I did

Ingredients

- 1 lb. russet potatoes, peeled

- 1/2 tsp kosher salt

- 2 tsp vegetable oil

- 1 pinch cayenne pepper

Instructions

- ❖ Slice segments into sticks too around 3/8 inch-wide.

- ❖ Cover potatoes with water and let boil for 5 minutes to discharge excess starches.

- ❖ Drain and cover with boiling water with several inches (or put in a bowl of boiling water). Let sit for 10 minutes.

- ❖ Drain potatoes and move onto several paper towels. Transfer to a mixing bowl drizzle with oil, season with cayenne, and toss to coat.

- ❖ Stack potatoes in a dual layer in the fryer basket. Slide out basket and throw fries; keep frying until golden brown, about 10 minutes longer. Toss chips with salt in a mixing bowl.

51. Cheese on Toast

Ingredients:

- Bread

- Garlic butter

- cayenne pepper

Method:

I'm going to show you how to make a really quick and easy cheese on toast. How I make my cheese on toast is I get the bread and I put garlic butter on each side of the bread.

For me this is a very important step. I then grate quite a generous amount of cheese and then sprinkle it over the top. I will also add a little dash of cayenne pepper on top. Pop into my air fryer on the pizza button so that is for eight minutes at 160 degrees. Once the time is up, it comes out perfect every single time with a real nice crunchy piece of toast.

52. Tomato Pork Chops

It is a rather quick and easy recipe.

Ingredients

- 1 bell pepper - sliced, your color option

- 1 (15 oz.) can tomato sauce

- garlic powder to flavor

- 4 pork chops

- 1 tsp, sliced

- pepper and salt to taste

Directions

- ❖ Dredge the pork chops in flour, add to the pan and brown well on both sides.

❖ Add the onion and bell pepper, stir and cook for 5 minutes in the air fryer, or until nearly tender. Return pork chops to skillet and pour into the sauce. Permit the sauce to begin bubbling and reduce heat.

❖ Simmer for half an hour and season with garlic powder, pepper and salt to taste.

53. Veggie Egg Bread

Ingredients:

- 1 tsp salt

- ½ pound cream cheese

- 10 eggs

- 4 cups grated zucchini

- 1 cup grated cheddar cheese

- ½ cup chopped tomatoes

- ½ tsp ground black pepper

- ½ cup sliced mushrooms, cooked

- ½ cup almond flour

- 2 tsp baking powder

Directions

❖ Be sure the pan will fit on your air fryer- normally a seven inch round pan will do the job flawlessly.

❖ Stir together the almond milk, pepper, salt and baking powder.

❖ In another bowl, beat the cream cheese until its smooth and nice afterward insert the eggs. Beat until well blended.

❖ Add the zucchini into the cream cheese mixture and stir until incorporated.

❖ Add the dry mix to the cream cheese jar and then stir well.

❖ Pour into the prepared pan and then cook at the fryer for 45 minutes

54.**Easy Muffins**

Ingredients:

- Sugar

- Butter

- Flour

- Eggs

- Milk

- Salt

Method:

We're going to make cupcakes. I have got a hundred grams of sugar, 250 grams of butter, 250 grams of flour, 4 eggs, a splash of milk and a dash of salt. We're just going to whisk this all up. I have got some of these cupcake holders. They're silicon ones. I'm going to add it to those and then we'll put them into the air fryer on the cupcake setting and let them cook away.

55. Almond Flour Pancake

Ingredients:

- 1 teaspoon vanilla extract

- 1 1/4 cup almond milk

- two Tbsp. granulated erythritol

- 1 teaspoon baking powder

- 2 eggs

- 1/2 cup whole milk

- 2 Tbsp. butter, melted

- 1/8 tsp salt

Directions

- ❖ Be sure the pan will fit on your air fryer- normally a seven inch round pan will do the job flawlessly.

- ❖ Put the eggs, butter, milk and vanilla extract in a blender and puree for around thirty minutes.

- ❖ Add the remaining ingredients into the blender and puree until smooth.

- ❖ Pour the pancake batter to the prepared pan and set from the fryer.

- ❖ Cook for 2 minutes or until the pancake is puffed and the top is gold brown.

- ❖ Slice and serve with keto sugar free!

56. Zucchini and Bacon Egg Bread

Ingredients:

- ½ cup almond flour

- 1 tsp salt

- ½ pound cream cheese

- 10 eggs

- 2 tsp baking powder

- ½ tsp ground black pepper

- 1 pound bacon cooked and crumbled

- 4 cups grated zucchini

- 1 cup grated cheddar cheese

Directions

❖ Be sure the pan will fit on your air fryer- normally a seven inch round pan will do the job flawlessly.

❖ Stir together the almond milk, pepper, salt and baking powder.

❖ In another bowl, beat the cream cheese until its smooth and nice afterward insert the eggs. Beat until well blended.

❖ Add the zucchini into the cream cheese mixture and stir until incorporated.

❖ Add the dry mix to the cream cheese jar and then stir well.

❖ Pour into the prepared pan and then cook at the fryer for 45 minutes

57. Raspberry Almond Pancake

Ingredients:

- 1/2 cup whole milk

- 2 Tbsp. butter, melted

- 1 teaspoon almond extract

- 2 eggs

- two Tbsp. granulated erythritol

- 1 teaspoon baking powder

- 1/8 tsp salt

- 1 1/4 cup almond milk

- 1/4 cup frozen or fresh desserts

Directions

I. Preheat your air fryer to 420 degrees F and line a baking pan using parchment paper. Be sure the pan will fit on your air fryer- normally a seven inch round pan will do the job flawlessly.

II. Put the eggs, butter, milk and almond extract in a blender and puree for around thirty minutes.

III. Add the remaining ingredients into the blender and puree until smooth.

IV. Pour the pancake batter to the pan and stir in the raspberries

V. Lightly.

VI. Put in the fryer.

VII. Slice and serve with keto sugar free!

58. Maple Brussel Sprout Chips

Ingredients:

- 2 Tbsp. olive oil

- 1 tsp sea salt

- 1 Pound Brussel Sprouts, ends removed

- 1 tsp maple extract

Method:

➤ Preheat your air fryer to 2400 degrees F and line the fryer tray with parchment paper.

➤ Peel the Brussels sprouts leaf at a time, putting the leaves in a massive bowl as you pare them.

➤ Toss the leaves using the olive oil, maple extract and salt then disperse onto the prepared tray.

➤ Bake for 15 minutes at the fryer, tossing halfway through to cook evenly.

➤ Serve warm or wrap in an airtight container after chilled.

59. Sweet and Tangy Apple Pork Chops

That is a recipe that I made using the thought that apples and pork go beautifully together! The seasonings provide the pork a pleasant and slightly spicy flavor. The apple cider increases the sweetness, while still bringing an exceptional tartness, since it's absorbed into the meat. Serve with applesauce, if wanted. Hope you like it!

Ingredients:

- 3 tbsp. brown sugar

- 1/2 tsp garlic powder

- 2 tbsp. honey mustard

- 1 tsp mustard powder

- 1/2 teaspoon ground cumin

- 1 lb. pork chops

- 2 tbsp. butter

- 1/2 tsp cayenne pepper (Optional)

- 3/4 cup apple cider

Instructions

- ❏ Mix brown sugar, honey mustard, mustard powder, cumin, cayenne pepper, and garlic powder together in a small bowl. Rub pork chops and let sit on a plate for flavors to split into pork chops, about 10 minutes.

- ❏ Melt butter in a large skillet over moderate heat; include apple cider. Organize coated pork chops from the skillet;

- ❏ Cook until pork chops are browned, 5 to 7 minutes each side.

60. Maple Brussel Sprout Chips

Ingredients:

- 2 Tbsp. olive oil

- 1 tsp sea salt

- 1 Pound Brussel Sprouts, ends removed

- 1 tsp maple extract

Method:

➤ Preheat your air fryer to 2400 degrees F and line the fryer tray with parchment paper.

➤ Peel the Brussels sprouts leaf at a time, putting the leaves in a massive bowl as you pare them.

➤ Toss the leaves using the olive oil, maple extract and salt then disperse onto the prepared tray.

➤ Bake for 15 minutes at the fryer, tossing halfway through to cook evenly.

➤ Serve warm or wrap in an airtight container after chilled.

61.Blueberry Pancake

Ingredients:

- 2 Tbsp. butter, melted

- 1 teaspoon vanilla extract

- 1 1/4 cup almond milk

- 2 eggs

- 1 teaspoon baking powder

- 1/8 tsp salt

- 1/4 cup frozen or fresh blueberries

- 1/2 cup whole milk

- Two Tbsp. granulated erythritol

Directions

1. Preheat your air fryer to 400 degrees F and line a baking pan using parchment paper. Be sure the pan will fit on your fryer- normally a seven inch round pan will do the job flawlessly.

2. Put the eggs, butter, milk and vanilla extract in a blender and puree for around thirty minutes.

3. Add the remaining ingredients into the blender and puree until smooth.

4. Pour the pancake batter to the pan and stir in the blueberries

5. Put in the fryer.

6. Slice and serve with keto sugar free!

62. Chocolate Croissants

Ingredients

- Puff pastry

- Flake chocolate

Method:

I wanted to show you how to make some chocolate croissants in your air fryer as well. So, what I have got here is one roll of puff pastry and then to go on top to make it chocolatey, I have got some flake chocolate. What I'm going to do is roll out my puff pastry and then I'm going to crumble some flake chocolates all over the pastry.

I'm then going to cut my pastry into eight. I'm going to cut them into fours and then I'll cut each four diagonally and then I'll roll them up into a croissant shape. Pop them into my air fryer, cook them on the muffin button which is a twelve minutes setting and then when they come out they are really really nice, chocolatey and delicious.

63.Strawberry Pancake

Ingredients:

- 1 teaspoon baking powder

- 1/8 tsp salt

- 1/4 cup fresh chopped tomatoes

- 2 eggs

- 1 teaspoon vanilla extract

- 1 1/4 cup almond milk

Directions

I.   Pre-heat the air fryer for around 15 minutes.

II.   Put the eggs, butter, milk and vanilla extract in a blender and simmer for about half an hour.

III.   Add the remaining ingredients into the blender and puree until smooth.

IV.   Pour the pancake batter to the pan and stir in the berries gently.

V.   Put in the fryer.

VI.   Slice and serve with keto sugar free!

64. Cheesy Zucchini Bake

Ingredients:

- 2 tsp baking powder

- ½ tsp ground black pepper

- 1 tsp salt

- ½ cup almond flour

- 4 cups grated zucchini

- ½ pound cream cheese

- 10 eggs

- 1 cup grated cheddar cheese

Method:

1. Be sure the pan will fit on your air fryer- normally a seven inch round pan will do the job flawlessly. If it's possible to fit a bigger pan, then do so!

2. Stir together the almond milk, pepper, salt and baking powder.

3. In another bowl beat the cream cheese until its smooth and nice afterward insert the eggs. Beat until well blended.

4. Add the zucchini into the cream cheese mixture and stir until incorporated.

5. Add the dry mix to the cream cheese jar and then stir well.

6. Pour into the prepared pan and then cook at the fryer for 45 minutes.

65. Basil-Garlic Grilled Pork Chops

I had been tired of the exact same old agendas, and opted to try out something new... WOW! These chops are excellent!! They're fantastic for casual entertaining or family dinner. Together with the fresh basil and grated garlic, the taste is quite refreshing! Everybody will adore these!

Ingredients

- 4 (8 ounce) pork chops

- 4 cloves garlic, minced

- ¼ cup chopped fresh basil

- 1 lime, juiced

- salt and black pepper to taste

Instructions

❖ Toss the pork chops with all the carrot juice in a bowl until evenly coated. Toss with ginger and garlic. Season the chops to taste with pepper and salt. Set aside to marinate for half an hour.

❖ Cook the pork chops on the fryer till no longer pink at the middle, 5 to 10 minutes each side.

66. Full English breakfast

Full English breakfast is one that my family really really likes. We have lived in England for a while so my kids really look forward to Saturday morning so that we make full English breakfast. However today I'm going to be showing you a special way to make it stress free.

I'm going to be starting off with the hash browns.

Ingredients:

- Potatoes

- Cheese

- Egg

- Salt

- Pepper

- Chili Flakes

- Sausage

Method:

So, the hash brownies are going to be composed of potatoes. I'm going to be using two, then I'm also going to be using cheese. This is shredded cheese and this is like the equivalent of one and a half cups of cheese. We are also going to be using one egg, this is one raw egg and some all-purpose flour, and this is the equivalent of two huge teaspoons of flour. We will be using some pepper along with chili flakes and finally of course some salt to taste. Right, so these are the ingredients that I'm going to be using for the hash browns.

Before we start off with hash browns let's move on to all the other ingredients or condiments that are going to make up the English breakfast so part of the traditional ones we also use would be the eggs so this will make up we're going to make sunny side up eggs I'm going to be using some tomatoes some sausage, so this is not this is not the same way you have a traditional English breakfast.

This isn't the same kind of way the sausage is or the way to slice but this is fine. Then we're going to be including baked beans right. So, this is a shop bought and actually there's still one more ingredient I'm going to be using: bacon. This is raw thinly sliced bacon and we have two slices of bread right. So, that's all the components or the condiments are going to go into the full English breakfast.

Let's start off straight away with the hash browns because all these other things are pretty much ready to go. Let's start with the preparation of the hash browns. So the first thing I'm going to be doing to grate the potatoes. With grated you can use any size. I want to use the really thin size because I want it more or less almost if it's already mashed or boiled. Because I'm going to be putting it in an array, I want it to take as little time as possible in order to get the potatoes done. If you've had English breakfast before let me know what you include or what you remove. I know people have different types of English breakfast at different times. Yeah, I know there's the black pudding, if you're a traditional English person you probably like black pudding instead.

We're done with the grating of the potatoes and I've rinsed it out in sense that I've put some water in. I'm giving it a good squeeze to make sure all the water is gone. This helps to remove the majority of the starch in the potatoes. So it's completely up to you, if you want to skip this process in the sense that you want to rinse out some of the water from the potatoes. Okay so that done, the next thing we're going to move on to the mixing. I'm going to put in my flour. This is two teaspoons but it seems like I'm going to use only one. Then I remember eggs, had a full raw egg for my potato to make the hash browns. I also have some cheese, add some salt to taste and some chili flakes. I like something hot and spicy and yeah that's why I add that. So, I give this a really good mix for hash browns, people usually sometimes add butter so it's completely up to you what you want to include in your own hash browns. I'm just keeping my own soft shots sweet and simple. You can add or subtract as much as you want.

I'm going to give my tray a spray just to oil it, because what I'm going to do guys, this is something different. I'm going to start off with the hash browns. I'm putting everything and it's going to come out like a cup sort of like a cupcake, because my cans are a bit deep. I'm going to spread it into two sections right because I want it to cook all the way through so the potatoes are going to come out, sort of like a cupcake or potato cups. I'm also going to give this another spray right now, this is different.

I'm going to put in oops my sausages right, to line them all in here. As I'm using the air fryer for everything stress less so hopefully this should work for a bachelor or spencer or a small family or just making breakfast for somebody for just one person in the family. This works pretty good. I'm going to put them in first so the next thing that is going to be included in the air fryer all three of them are going in now is the bacon. I'm going to put the bacon this way, alternatively, I could have chopped up the bacon and put them in one of these sections. Maybe I would actually just do that so that you have a look-see at its rest of the bacon. I'm just going to cut this one in here.

Throw it into the extra bit there again, I'm not going to be bothered about these bacon, because you know they're going to come up with their own oil. It's going to go into the air fryer oven. Put it in the air fryer oven and let it fry just turning the timer to one hour. It's an air fryer oven and the specific degree setting should be up on your screen and yeah so once this is ready again, like I said it's halfway into the cooking of the sausages of the hash browns and the bacon.

I'm now going to include the baked beans and the eggs because those ones will actually take less time compared to what you've got in the oven. I've had these in the air fryer and I can see that my bacon is coming out nicely.

You see that so it depends on you if this is how you like your bacons this is the point in which you take them out. So, I'm just going to chuck the monotone section of the cupcake bits. What I'm going to do is to put the ones that are under done on the top and the ones that are already getting as crisp, I'm going to put them at the bottom. Now I'm just trying to get my stuff together. I'm scooping out all the sausages tone section so that I have two sections free for me to put my eggs and my baked beans. I'm going to have the egg sunny side up, I'm not going to spray the container again because all the bacon oil is in the egg, is in the cupcake holder. I'm just going to break two eggs and putting two into one section and then add some salt and some chili flakes. Our egg begins to cool, then I'm also going to put in the baked beans right in the final section. We are all good to go so I just want to show you guys what it looks like.

We've got the eggs we've got the baked beans we've got everything in the section in the containers. I'm going to have the the tomatoes, I'm just going to line them on top here and yeah voila. I know for some people it's a lot of work but this is really stress less. The only bit where you have lots of work to do is with the grating of the potatoes and that's pretty much it. We're going to allow these now to cook all the way through by the time the egg is done and the baked paint is ready, the entire dish should be ready. We're about 30 minutes into the entire thing and it's looking really really good. I just want to bring this and mix up the sausages a bit, yeah and put this back because you need a couple of minutes to go. You can see the egg, you can see the bacon everything is looking wonderful. I'm going to move this all the way back because I want to put my tomatoes just to give it a little bit of somehow grilled max and then my bread right just to heat it up.

Let it give me somewhat like a mini toast. I'm going to shut this down now its done 30 minutes and it's done right. I'm not looking to get toasted bread but I just want this really warm. It's not toasted but it's warm and really crispy. I'm going to get the bread out of the way and the same thing with the tomatoes. So they're just warm so that when the breakfast is being eaten it's really nice and warm and fuzzy. Let's get onto plating it okay we are all ready, can you see that looks really good so and this is every single thing in one place right. So, our potatoes looks properly cooked a bit hot, our hash browns potatoes looks good and you can see our sausages. It did really really well cooked properly right and the same thing with the bacon so you can see all crispy or crunchy. I was able to achieve breakfast.

It took me about 30 minutes to make the entire dish so you can see my eggs yummy yummy yummy. I'm just going to dish this out and yeah so you can see the entire dish all presented for you. This is our English breakfast right you have the bread, we've got the bacon, I'm going to put in the sausages. This is a wonderful breakfast. All I really did was just to check it up at various times and baked beans is ready. This could actually is pretty decent meal and I think can it's perfect for more than one person. We have got egg there's not mushroom, there is no black pudding but this is completely fine the way it is right. So, this is what our full English breakfast looks like on some days and I've got the eggs, I've got the bacon, I still have some bacon there in the tray because I did make a lot so, still have some eggs.

I have got some bacon some bread, yeah with a glass of milk or a cup of coffee you're good to go.

67. Garlic Brussel Sprout Chips

Ingredients:

- 1 tsp sea salt

- 1 Pound Brussel Sprouts, ends removed

- 2 Tbsp. olive oil

- 1 tsp garlic powder

Method:

❖ Preheat your air fryer to 2400 degrees F and line the fryer tray with parchment paper.

❖ Peel the Brussels sprouts leaf at a time, putting the leaves in a massive bowl as you pare them.

❖ Toss the leaves together with olive oil, garlic powder and salt then disperse onto the prepared tray.

❖ Bake for 15 minutes at the fryer, tossing halfway through to cook evenly.

68.Home and Asparagus

Ingredients:

- 1/4 teaspoon ground black pepper

- 1/4 tsp salt

- 1 lb. asparagus spears

Directions

- ❏ Preheat your air fryer to 400 degrees F and line your fryer tray using a

- ❏ Set the cod filets onto the parchment and sprinkle with the pepper and salt and rub the spices to the fish.

- ❏ Top the fish with the remaining components then wrap the parchment paper around the fish filets, surrounding them entirely.

- ❏ Put the tray in the fryer and bake for 20 minutes.

69.Herbed Parmesan Crackers

Ingredients:

- 2 Tbsp. Italian seasoning

- ½ cup chia seeds

- 1 ½ cups sunflower seeds

- 1 egg

- 2 Tbsp. butter, melted

- Salt

- ½ tsp garlic powder

- ½ tsp baking powder

- ¾ cup parmesan cheese, grated

Method:

❏ Set the sunflower seeds and chia seeds in a food processor until finely mixed to a powder. Put into a large bowl.

❏ Add the cheese, Italian seasoning, garlic powder and baking powder to the bowl and combine well.

❏ Add the melted butter and egg and stir till a wonderful dough forms.

❏ Put the dough onto a sheet of parchment and then put the following slice of parchment on top.

❏ Roll the dough into a thin sheet around 1/8 inch thick.

❏ Remove the top piece of parchment and lift the dough with the underside parchment and set onto a sheet tray which can fit in the air fryer.

❏ Score the cracker dough to your desired shape and bake for 40-45cminutes.

❏ Break the crackers aside and enjoy!

70.Salmon and Asparagus

Ingredients:

- ¼ tsp ground black pepper

- 1 ¾ pound salmon fillets

- ¼ tsp salt

- 1 pound asparagus spears

- 1 Tbsp. lemon juice

- 1 Tbsp. fresh chopped parsley

- 3 Tbsp. olive oil

Method

→ Preheat your air fryer to 400 degrees F and line your fryer tray using a long piece of parchment paper.

→ Set the salmon filets onto the parchment and sprinkle with the salt and pepper and rub the spices to the fish.

→ Top the fish with the rest of the ingredients then wrap the parchment paper around the fish filets, surrounding them completely.

→ Put the tray in the fryer and bake for 20 minutes.

71.Super Seed Parmesan Crackers

Ingredients:

- ½ tsp baking powder

- 1 egg

- 2 Tbsp. butter, melted

- 1 cups sunflower seeds

- ¾ cup parmesan cheese, grated

- 2 Tbsp. Italian seasoning

- ½ cup chia seeds

- ½ cup hulled hemp seeds

- ½ tsp garlic powder

- Salt

Method:

★ Preheat your air fryer to 300 degrees F.

★ Put into a large bowl.

★ Add the cheese, Italian seasoning, garlic powder and baking powder to the bowl and combine well.

★ Add the melted butter and egg and stir till a wonderful dough forms.

★ Put the dough onto a sheet of parchment and then put the following slice of parchment on top.

★ Roll the dough into a thin sheet around 1/8 inch thick.

★ Remove the top piece of parchment and lift the dough with the underside parchment and set onto a sheet tray which will fit from the air fryer.

★ Score the cracker dough to your desired shape and bake for 40-45 minutes.

★ Break the crackers aside and enjoy!

Conclusion

We have included 70 best recipes for you in this book. So, just try it out and then give us feedback with images of cooking.

The Complete Air Fryer Cookbook with Pictures

70+ Perfectly Portioned Air Fryer Recipes for Busy People on a Budget

By Michelle Polpetta

Contents

INTRODUCTION:

The aim of this cookbook is to provide the easiness for those who are professional or doing job somewhere. But with earning, it is also quite necessary to cook food easily & timely instead of ordering hygienic or costly junk food. As we know, after doing office work, no one can cook food with the great effort. For the ease of such people, there are a lot of latest advancements in kitchen accessories. The most popular kitchen appliances usually helps to make foods or dishes like chicken, mutton, beef, potato chips and many other items in less time and budget. There are a lot of things that should be considered when baking with an air fryer. One of the most important tips is to make sure you have all of your equipment ready for the bake. It is best to be prepared ahead of time and this includes having pans, utensils, baking bags, the air fryer itself, and the recipe book instead of using stove or oven. With the help of an air fryer, you can make various dishes for a single person as well as the entire family timely and effortlessly. As there is a famous proverb that "Nothing can be done on its own", it indicates that every task takes time for completion. Some tasks take more time and effort and some requires less time and effort for their completion. Therefore, with the huge range of advancements that come to us are just for our ease. By using appliances like an air fryer comes for the comfort of professional people who are busy in earning their livelihood. In this book, you can follow the latest, delicious, and quick, about 70 recipes that will save your time and provide you healthy food without any great effort.

Chapter # 1:

An Overview & Benefits of an Air Fryer

Introduction:

The most popular kitchen appliance that usually helps to make foods or dishes like chicken, mutton, beef, potato chips and many other items in less time and budget.

Today, everything is materialistic, every person is busy to earn great livelihood. Due to a huge burden of responsibilities, they have no time to cook food on stove after doing hard work. Because, traditionally cooking food on the stove takes more time and effort. Therefore, there are a vast variety of Kitchen appliances. The kitchen appliances are so much helpful in making or cooking food in few minutes and in less budget. You come to home from job, and got too much tired. So, you can cook delicious food in an Air Fryer efficiently and timely as compared to stove. You can really enjoy the food without great effort and getting so much tired.

The Air Fryer Usability:

Be prepared to explore all about frying foods that you learned. To crisp, golden brown excellence (yes, French-fried potatoes and potato chips!), air fryers will fry your favourite foods using minimum or no oil. You can not only make commonly fried foods such as chips and French fries of potatoes, however it is also ideal for proteins, vegetables such as drummettes and chicken wings, coquettes & feta triangles as well as appetizers. And cookies are perfectly cooked in an air fryer, such as brownies and blondies.

The Air Fryer Works as:

- Around 350-375°F (176-190°C) is the ideal temperature of an Air Fryer

- To cook the surface of the food, pour over a food oil at the temperature mentioned above. The oil can't penetrate because it forms a type of seal.
- Simultaneously, the humidity within the food turns into steam that helps to actually cook the food from the inside. It is cleared that the steam helps to maintain the oil out of the food.
- The oil flows into the food at a low temperature, rendering it greasy.
- It oxidizes the oil and, at high temperatures, food will dry out.

On the other hand, an air fryer is similar to a convection oven, but in a diverse outfit, food preparation done at very high temperatures whereas, inside it, dry air circulates around the food at the same time, while making it crisp without putting additional fat, it makes it possible for cooking food faster.

What necessary to Search for in an Air Fryer?

As we know, several different sizes and models of air fryers are available now. If you're cooking for a gathering, try the extra-large air fryer, that can prepare or fry a whole chicken, other steaks or six servings of French fries.

Suppose, you've a fixed counter space, try the Large Air Fryer that uses patented machinery to circulate hot air for sufficient, crispy results. The latest air fryer offers an extra compact size with identical capacity! and tar equipment, which ensures that food is cooking evenly (no further worries of build-ups). You will be able to try all the fried foods you enjoy, with no embarrassment.

To increase the functionality of an air fryer, much more, you can also purchase a wide range of different accessories, including a stand, roasting pan, muffin cups, and mesh baskets. Check out the ingredients of our air fryer we created, starting from buttermilk with black pepper seasoning to fry chicken or Sichuan garlic seasoning suitable for Chinese cuisine.

We will read about the deep fryer, with tips and our favourite recipes like burgers, chicken wings, and many more.

Most Common - Five Guidelines for an Air Fryer usage:

1. Shake the food.

Open the air fryer and shake the foods efficiently because the food is to "fry" in the machine's basket—Light dishes like Sweet French fries and Garlic chips will compress. Give Rotation to the food every 5-10 mins for better performance

2. Do not overload.

Leave enough space for the food so that the air circulates efficiently; so that's gives you crunchy effects. Our kitchen testing cooks trust that the snacks and small batches can fry in air fryer.

3. Slightly spray to food.

Gently spray on food by a cooking spray bottle and apply a touch of oil on food to make sure the food doesn't stick to the basket.

4. Retain an Air fry dry.

Beat food to dry before start cooking (even when marinated, e.g.) to prevent splashing & excessive smoke. Likewise, preparing high-fat foods such as chicken steaks or wings, be assured to remove the grease from the lower part of machine regularly.

5. Other Most Dominant cooking techniques.

The air fryer is not just for deep frying; It is also perfect for further safe methods of cooking like baking, grilling, roasting and many more. Our kitchen testing really loves using the unit for cooking salmon in air fryer!

An Air Fryer Helps to reduce fat content

Generally, food cooked in deep fryer contains higher fat level than preparing food in other cooking appliances. For Example; a fried chicken breast contains about 30% more fat just like a fat level in roasted chicken

Many Manufacturers claimed, an Air fryer can reduce fat from fried food items up-to 75%. So, an air fryer requires less amount of fat than a deep fryer. As, many dishes cooked in deep fryer consume 75% oil (equal to 3 cups) and an air fryer prepare food by applying the oil in just about 1 tablespoon (equal to 15ml).

One research tested the potato chips prepared in air fryer characteristics then observed: the air frying method produces a final product with slightly lower fat but same moisture content and color. So, there is a major impact on anyone's health, an excessive risk of illnesses such as inflammation, infection and heart disease has been linked to a greater fat intake from vegetable oils.

Air Fryer provides an Aid in Weight Loss

The dishes prepared deep fryer are not just having much fat but also more in calories that causes severe increase in weight. Another research of 33,542 Spanish grown-ups indicates that a greater usage of fried food linked with a higher occurrence of obesity. Dietetic fat has about twice like many calories per gram while other macro-nutrients such as carbohydrates, vitamins and proteins, averaging in at 9 calories throughout each and every gram of oil or fat.

By substituting to air fryer is an easy way to endorse in losing weight and to reduce calories and it will be done only by taking food prepared in air fryer.

Air Fried food may reduce the potentially harmful chemicals

Frying foods can produce potentially hazardous compounds such as acrylamide, in contrast to being higher in fat and calories. An acrylamide is a compound that is formed in carbohydrate- rich dishes or foods during highly-heated cooking methods such as frying. Acrylamide is known as a "probable carcinogen" which indicates as some research suggests that it could be associated with the development of cancer. Although the findings are conflicting, the link between dietary acrylamide and a greater risk of kidney, endometrial and ovarian cancers has been identified in some reports. Instead of cooking food in a deep fryer, air frying your food may aid the acrylamide content. Some researches indicates that air-frying method may cut the acrylamide by 90% by comparing deep frying method. All other extremely harmful chemicals produced by high-heat cooking are polycyclic aromatic hydrocarbons, heterocyclic amines and aldehydes and may be associated with a greater risk of cancer. That's why, the air fried food may help to reduce the chance of extremely dangerous chemicals or compounds and maintain your health.

Chapter # 2:

70 Perfectly Portioned Air Fryer Recipes for Busy People in Minimum Budget

1. Air fried corn, zucchini and haloumi fritters

Ingredients

- Coarsely grated block haloumi - 225g
- Coarsely grated Zucchini - 2 medium sized
- Frozen corn kernels - 150g (1 cup)
- Lightly whisked eggs - 2
- Self-raising flour - 100g
- Extra virgin olive oil - to drizzle
- Freshly chopped oregano leaves - 3 tablespoons
- Fresh oregano extra sprigs - to serve
- Yoghurt - to serve

Method

1. Use your palms to squeeze out the extra liquid from the zucchini and place them in a bowl. Add the corn and haloumi and stir for combining them. Then add the eggs, oregano and flour. Add seasoning and stir until fully mixed.

2. Set the temperature of an air fryer to 200 C. Put spoonsful of the mixture of zucchini on an air fryer. Cook until golden and crisp, for 8 minutes. Transfer to a dish that is clean. Again repeat this step by adding the remaining mixture in 2 more batches.

3. Take a serving plate and arrange soft fritters on it. Take yoghurt in a small serving bowl. Add seasoning of black pepper on the top of yoghurt. Drizzle with olive oil. At the end, serve this dish with extra oregano.

2. Air fryer fried rice

Ingredients

- Microwave long grain rice - 450g packet
- Chicken tenderloins - 300g
- Rindless bacons - 4 ranchers
- Light Soy sauce - 2 tablespoons
- Oyster sauce - 2 tablespoons
- Sesame oil - 1 tablespoon
- Fresh finely grated ginger - 3 tablespoons
- Frozen peas - 120g (3/4 cup)
- Lightly whisked eggs - 2
- Sliced green shallots - 2
- Thin sliced red chilli - 1
- Oyster sauce - to drizzle

Method

1. Set the 180°C temperature of an air fryer. Bacon and chicken is placed on the rack of an air fryer. Cook them until fully cooked for 8-10 minutes. Shift it to a clean plate and set this plate aside to cool. Then, slice and chop the bacon and chicken.

2. In the meantime, separate the rice grains in the packet by using your fingers. Heat the rice for 60 seconds in a microwave. Shift to a 20cm ovenproof, round high-sided pan or dish. Apply the sesame oil, soy sauce, ginger, oyster sauce and 10ml water and mix well.

3. Put a pan/dish in an air fryer. Cook the rice for 5 minutes till them soft. Then whisk the chicken, half of bacon and peas in the eggs. Completely cook the eggs in 3 minutes. Mix and season the top of half shallot with white pepper and salt.

4. Serve with the seasoning of chilli, remaining bacon and shallot and oyster sauce.

3. Air fried banana muffins

Ingredients

- Ripe bananas - 2
- Brown sugar - 60g (1/3 cup)
- Olive oil - 60ml (1/4 cup)
- Buttermilk - 60ml (1/4 cup)

- Self-raising flour - 150g (1 cup)
- Egg - 1
- Maple syrup - to brush or to serve

Method

1. Mash the bananas in a small bowl using a fork. Until needed, set aside.

2. In a medium cup, whisk the flour and sugar using a balloon whisk. In the middle, make a well. Add the buttermilk, oil and egg. Break up the egg with the help of a whisk. Stir by using wooden spoon until the mixture is mixed. Stir the banana through it.

3. Set the temperature of an air fryer at 180C. Splits half of the mixture into 9 cases of patties. Remove the rack from the air fryer and pass the cases to the rack carefully. Switch the rack back to the fryer. Bake the muffins completely by cooking them for 10 minutes. Move to the wire rack. Repeat this step on remaining mixture to produce 18 muffins.

4. Brush the muffin tops with maple syrup while they're still warm. Serve, if you like, with extra maple syrup.

4. Air fried Nutella brownies

Ingredients

- Plain flour - 150g (1 cup)

- Castor white sugar - 225g (1 cup)
- Lightly whisked eggs - 3
- Nutella - 300g (1 cup)
- Cocoa powder - to dust

Method

1. Apply butter in a 20cm circular cake pan. Cover the base by using baking paper.

2. Whisk the flour and sugar together in a bowl by using balloon whisk. In the middle, make a well. Add the Nutella and egg in the middle of bowl by making a well. Stir with a large metal spoon until mixed. Move this mixture to the previously prepared pan and smooth the surface of the mixture by using metal spoon.

3. Pre - heat an air fryer to 160C. Bake the brownie about 40 minutes or until a few crumbs stick out of a skewer inserted in the middle. Fully set aside to cool.

4. Garnish the top of the cake by dusting them with cocoa powder, and cut them into pieces. Brownies are ready to be served.

5. Air fried celebration bites

Ingredients

- Frozen shortcrust partially thawed pastry - 4 sheets

- Lightly whisked eggs - 1
- Unrapped Mars Celebration chocolates - 24
- Icing sugar - to dust
- Cinnamon sugar - to dust
- Whipped cream - to serve

Method

1. Slice each pastry sheet into 6 rectangles. Brush the egg gently. One chocolate is placed in the middle of each rectangular piece of pastry. Fold the pastry over to cover the chocolate completely. Trim the pastry, press and seal the sides. Place it on a tray containing baking paper. Brush the egg on each pastry and sprinkle cinnamon sugar liberally.

2. In the air-fryer basket, put a sheet of baking paper, making sure that the paper is 1 cm smaller than the basket to allow airflow. Put six pockets in the basket by taking care not to overlap. Cook for 8-9 minutes at 190°C until pastries are completely cooked with golden color. Shift to a dish. Free pockets are then used again.

3. Sprinkle Icing sugar on the top of tasty bites. Serve them with a whipped cream to intensify its flavor.

6. Air fried nuts and bolts

Ingredients

- Dried farfalle pasta - 2 cups
- Extra virgin olive oil - 60ml (1/4th cup)
- Brown sugar - 2 tablespoons
- Onion powder - 1 tablespoon
- Smoked paprika - 2 tablespoons
- Chili powder - 1/2 tablespoon
- Garlic powder - 1/2 tablespoon
- Pretzels - 1 cup
- Raw macadamias - 80g (1/2 cup)
- Raw cashews - 80g (1/2 cup)
- Kellog's Nutri-grain cereal - 1 cup
- Sea salt - 1 tablespoon

Method

1. Take a big saucepan of boiling salted water, cook the pasta until just ready and soft. Drain thoroughly. Shift pasta to a tray and pat with a paper towel to dry. Move the dried pasta to a wide pot.

2. Mix the sugar, oil, onion, paprika, chili and garlic powders together in a clean bowl. Add half of this mixture in the bowl containing pasta. Toss this bowl slightly for the proper coating of mixture over pasta.

3. Set the temperature at 200C of an Air Fryer. Put the pasta in air fryer's pot. After cooking for 5 minutes, shake the pot and cook for more 5-7 minutes, until they look golden and crispy. Shift to a wide bowl.

4. Take the pretzels in a bowl with the nuts and apply the remaining mixture of spices. Toss this bowl for the proper coating. Put in air fryer's pot and cook at 180C for 3-4 minutes. Shake this pot and cook for more 2-3 minutes until it's golden in color. First add pasta and then add the cereal. Sprinkle salt on it and toss to mix properly. Serve this dish after proper cooling.

7. Air fried coconut shrimps

Ingredients

- Plain flour - 1/2 cup
- Eggs - 2
- Bread crumbs - 1/2 cup
- Black pepper powder - 1.5 teaspoons
- Sweetless flaked coconut - 3/4 cup
- Uncooked, deveined and peeled shrimp - 12 ounces
- Salt - 1/2 teaspoon
- Honey - 1/4 cup
- Lime juice - 1/4 cup
- Finely sliced serrano chili - 1
- Chopped cilantro - 2 teaspoons
- Cooking spray

Method

1. Stir the pepper and flour in a clean bowl together. Whisk the eggs in another bowl and h panko and coconut in separate bowl. Coat the shrimps with flour mixture by holding each shrimp by tail and shake off the extra flour. Then coat the floured shrimp with egg and allow it to drip off excess. Give them the final coat of coconut mixture and press them to stick. Shift on a clean plate. Spray shrimp with cooking oil.

2. Set the temperature of the air-fryer to 200C. In an air fryer, cook half of the shrimp for 3 minutes. Turn the shrimp and cook further for more 3 minutes until color changes in golden. Use 1/4 teaspoon of salt for seasoning. Repeat this step for the rest of shrimps.

3. In the meantime, prepare a dip by stirring lime juice, serrano chili and honey in a clean bowl.

4. Serve fried shrimps with sprinkled cilantro and dip.

8. Air fried Roasted Sweet and Spicy Carrots

Ingredients

- Cooking oil
- Melted butter - 1 tablespoon
- Grated orange zest - 1 teaspoon
- Carrots - 1/2 pound
- Hot honey - 1 tablespoon
- Cardamom powder - 1/2 teaspoon
- Fresh orange juice - 1 tablespoon
- Black pepper powder - to taste
- Salt - 1 pinch

Method

1. Set the temperature of an air to 200C. Lightly coat its pot with cooking oil.

2. Mix honey, cardamom and orange zest in a clean bowl. Take 1 tablespoon of this sauce in another bowl and place aside. Coat carrots completely by tossing them in remaining sauce. Shift carrots to an air fryer pot.

3. Air fry the carrots and toss them after every 6 minutes. Cook carrots for 15-20 minutes until they are fully cooked and roasted. Combine honey butter sauce with orange juice to make sauce. Coat carrots with this sauce. Season with black pepper and salt and serve this delicious dish.

9. Air fried Chicken Thighs

Ingredients

- Boneless chicken thighs - 4
- Extra virgin olive oil - 2 teaspoons
- Smoked paprika - 1 teaspoon
- Salt - 1/2 teaspoon
- Garlic powder - 3/4 teaspoon
- Black pepper powder - 1/2 teaspoon

Method

1. Set the temperature of an air fryer to 200C.

2. Dry chicken thighs by using tissue paper. Brush olive oil on the skin side of each chicken thigh. Shift the single layer of chicken thighs on a clean tray.

3. Make a mixture of salt, black pepper, paprika and garlic powder in a clean bowl. Use a half of this mixture for the seasoning of 4 chicken thighs on both sides evenly. Then shift single layer of chicken thighs in an air fryer pot by placing skin side up.

4. Preheat the air fryer and maintain its temperature to 75C. Fry chicken for 15-18 minutes until its water become dry and its color changes to brown. Serve immediately.

10. Air fried French Fries

Ingredients

- Peeled Potatoes - 1 pound
- Vegetable oil - 2 tablespoon
- Cayenne pepper - 1 pinch
- Salt - 1/2 teaspoon

Method

1. Lengthwise cut thick slices of potato of 3/8 inches.

2. Soak sliced potatoes for 5 minutes in water. Drain excess starch water from soaked potatoes after 5 minutes. Place these potatoes in boiling water pan for 8-10 minutes.

3. Remove water from the potatoes and dry them completely. Cool them for 10 minutes and shift in a clean bowl. Add some oil and fully coat the potatoes with cayenne by tossing.

4. Set the temperature of an air fryer to 190C. Place two layers of potatoes in air fryer pot and cook them for 10-15 minutes. Toss fries continuously and cook for more 10 minutes until their color changes to golden brown. Season fries with salt and serve this appetizing dish immediately.

11. Air fried Mini Breakfast Burritos

Ingredients

- Mexican style chorizo - 1/4 cup
- Sliced potatoes - 1/2 cup
- Chopped serrano pepper - 1
- 8-inch flour tortillas - 4
- Bacon grease - 1 tablespoon
- Chopped onion - 2 tablespoon
- Eggs - 2
- Cooking avacado oil - to spray
- Salt - to taste
- Black pepper powder - to taste

Method

1. Take chorizo in a large size pan and cook on medium flame for 8 minutes with continuous stirring until its color change into reddish brown. Shift chorizo in a clean plate and place separate.

2. Take bacon grease in same pan and melt it on medium flame. Place sliced potatoes and cook them for 10 minutes with constant stirring. Add serrano pepper and onion meanwhile. Cook for more 2-5 minutes until potatoes are fully cooked, onion and serrano pepper become soften. Then add chorizo and eggs and cook for more 5 minutes until potato mixture is fully incorporated. Use pepper and salt for seasoning.

3. In the meantime, heat tortillas in a large pan until they become soft and flexible. Put 1/3 cup of chorizo mixture at the center of each tortilla. Filling is covered by rolling the upper and lower side of tortilla and give shape of burrito. Spray cooking oil and place them in air fryer pot.

4. Fry these burritos at 200C for 5 minutes. Change the side's continuously and spray with cooking oil. Cook in air fryer for 3-4 minutes until color turns into light brown. Shift burritos in a clean dish and serve this delicious dish.

12. Air fried Vegan Tator Tots

Ingredients

- Frozen potato nuggets (Tator Tots) - 2 cups
- Buffalo wing sauce - 1/4 cup
- Vegan ranch salad - 1/4 cup

Method

1. Set the temperature of an air fryer to 175C.

2. Put frozen potato nuggets in air fryer pot and cook for 6-8 minutes with constant shake.

3. Shift potatoes to a large-sized bowl and add wing sauce. Combine evenly by tossing them and place them again in air fryer pot.

4. Cook more for 8-10 minutes without disturbance. Shift to a serving plate. Serve with ranch dressing and enjoy this dish.

13. Air fried Roasted Cauliflower

Ingredients

- Cauliflower florets - 4 cups
- Garlic - 3 cloves
- Smoked paprika - 1/2 teaspoon
- Peanut oil - 1 tablespoon
- Salt - 1/2 teaspoon

Method

1. Set the temperature of an air fryer to 200C.

2. Smash garlic cloves with a knife and mix with salt, oil and paprika. Coat cauliflower in this mixture.

3. Put coated cauliflower in air fryer pot and cook around 10-15 minutes with stirring after every 5 minutes. Cook according to desired color and crispiness and serve immediately.

14. Air fried Cinnamon-Sugar Doughnuts

Ingredients

- White sugar - 1/2 cup
- Brown sugar - 1/4 cup
- Melted butter - 1/4 cup
- Cinnamon powder - 1 teaspoon
- Ground nutmeg - 1/4 TEASPOON
- Packed chilled flaky biscuit dough - 1 (16.3 ounce)

Method

1. Put melted butter in a clean bowl. Add brown sugar, white sugar, nutmeg and cinnamon and mix.

2. Divide and cut biscuit dough into many single biscuits and give them the shape of doughnuts using a biscuit cutter. Shift doughnuts in an air fryer pot.

3. Air fry the doughnuts for 5-6 minutes at 175C until color turns into golden brown. Turn the side of doughnuts and cook for more 1-3 minutes.

4. Shift doughnuts from air fryer to a clean dish and dip them in melted butter. Then completely coat these doughnuts in sugar and cinnamon mixture and serve frequently.

15. Air Fried Broiled Grapefruit

Ingredients

- Chilled red grapefruit - 1
- Melted butter - 1 tablespoon
- Brown sugar - 2 tablespoon
- Ground cinnamon - 1/2 teaspoon
- Aluminium foil

Method

1. Set the temperature of an air fryer to 200C.

2. Cut grapefruit crosswise to half and also cut a thin slice from one end of grapefruit for sitting your fruit flat on a plate.

3. Mix brown sugar in melted butter in a small sized bowl. Coat the cut side of the grapefruit with this mixture. Dust the little brown sugar over it.

4. Take 2 five inch pieces of aluminium foil and put the half grapefruit on each piece. Fold the sides evenly to prevent juice leakage. Place them in air fryer pot.

5. Broil for 5-7 minutes until bubbling of sugar start in an air fryer. Before serving, sprinkle cinnamon on grapefruit.

16. Air Fried Brown Sugar and Pecan Roasted Apples

Ingredients

- Apples - 2 medium
- Chopped pecans - 2 tablespoons
- Plain flour - 1 teaspoon
- Melted butter - 1 tablespoon
- Brown sugar - 1 tablespoon
- Apple pie spice - 1/4 teaspoon

Method
1. Set the temperature of an air fryer to 180C.

2. Mix brown sugar, pecan, apple pie spice and flour in a clean bowl. Cut apples in wedges and put them in another bowl and coat them with melted butter by tossing. Place a single layer in an air fryer pot and add mixture of pecan on the top.

3. Cook apples for 12-15 minutes until they get soft.

17. Air Fried Breaded Sea Scallops

Ingredients

- Crushed butter crackers - 1/2 cup
- Seafood seasoning - 1/2 teaspoon
- Sea scallops - 1 pound
- Garlic powder - 1/2 teaspoon
- Melted butter - 2 tablespoons
- Cooking oil - for spray

Method

1. Set the temperature of an air fryer to 198C.

2. Combine garlic powder, seafood seasoning and cracker crumbs in a clean bowl. Take melted butter in another bowl.

3. Coat each scallop with melted butter. Then roll them in breading until completely enclose. Place them on a clean plate and repeat this step with rest of the scallops.

4. Slightly spray scallops with cooking oil and place them on the air fryer pot at equal distance. You may work in 2-3 batches.

5. Cook them for 2-3 minutes in preheated air fryer. Use a spatula to change the side of each scallop. Cook for more 2 minutes until they become opaque. Dish out in a clean plate and serve immediately.

18. Air Fried Crumbed Fish

Ingredients

- Flounder fillets - 4
- Dry bread crumbs - 1 cup
- Egg - 1
- Sliced lemon - 1
- Vegetable oil - 1/4 cup

Method

1. Set the temperature of an air fryer to 180C.

2. Combine oil and bread crumbs in a clean bowl and mix them well.

3. Coat each fish fillets with beaten egg, then evenly dip them in the crumbs mixture.

4. Place coated fillets in preheated air fryer and cook for 10-12 minutes until fish easily flakes by touching them with fork. Shift prepared fish in a clean plate and serve with lemon slices.

19. Air Fried Cauliflower and Chickpea Tacos

Ingredients

- Cauliflower - 1 small
- Chickpeas - 15 ounce
- Chili powder - 1 teaspoon
- Cumin powder - 1 teaspoon
- Lemon juice - 1 tablespoon
- Sea salt - 1 teaspoon
- Garlic powder - 1/4 teaspoon
- Olive oil - 1 tablespoon

Method

1. Set the temperature of an air fryer to 190C.

2. Mix lime juice, cumin, garlic powder, salt, olive oil and chili powder in a clean bowl. Now coat well the cauliflower and chickpeas in this mixture by constant stirring.

3. Put cauliflower mixture in an air fryer pot. Cook for 8-10 minutes with constant stirring. Cook for more 10 minutes and stir for final time. Cook for more 5 minutes until desired crispy texture is attained.

5. Place cauliflower mixture by using spoon and serve.

20. Air Fried Roasted Salsa

Ingredients

- Roma tomatoes - 4
- Seeded Jalapeno pepper - 1

- Red onion - 1/2
- Garlic - 4 cloves
- Cilantro - 1/2 cup
- Lemon juice - 1
- Cooking oil - to spray
- Salt - to taste

Method

1. Set the temperature of an air fryer to 200C.

2. Put tomatoes, red onion and skin side down of jalapeno in an air fryer pot. Brush lightly these vegetables with cooking oil for roasting them easily.

3. Cook vegetables in an air fryer for 5 minutes. Then add garlic cloves and again spray with cooking oil and fry for more 5 minutes.

4. Shift vegetables to cutting board and allow them to cool for 8-10 minutes.

5. Separate skins of jalapeno and tomatoes and chop them with onion into large pieces. Add them to food processor bowl and add lemon juice, cilantro, garlic and

salt. Pulsing for many times until all the vegetables are evenly chopped. Cool them for 10-15 minutes and serve this delicious dish immediately.

21. Air Fried Flour Tortilla Bowls

Ingredients

- Flour tortilla - 1 (8 inch)
- Souffle dish - 1 (4 1/2 inch)

Method

1. Set the temperature of an air fryer to 190C.

2. Take tortilla in a large pan and heat it until it become soft. Put tortilla in the souffle dish by patting down side and fluting up from its sides of dish.

3. Air fry tortilla for 3-5 minutes until its color change into golden brown.

4. Take out tortilla bowl from the dish and put the upper side in the pot. Air fry again for more 2 minutes until its color turns into golden brown. Dish out and serve.

22. Air Fried Cheese and Mini Bean Tacos

Ingredients

- Can Refried beans - 16 ounce
- American cheese - 12 slices
- Flour tortillas - 12 (6 inch)
- Taco seasoning mix - 1 ounce
- Cooking oil - to spray

Method

1. Set the temperature of an air fryer to 200C.

2. Combine refried beans and taco seasoning evenly in a clean bowl and stir.

3. Put 1 slice of cheese in the center of tortilla and place 1 tablespoon of bean mixture over cheese. Again place second piece of cheese over this mixture. Fold tortilla properly from upper side and press to enclose completely. Repeat this step for the rest of beans, cheese and tortillas.

4. Spray cooking oil on the both sides of tacos. Put them in an air fryer at equal distance. Cook the tacos for 3 minutes and turn it side and again cook for more 3 minutes. Repeat this step for the rest of tacos. Transfer to a clean plate and serve immediately.

23. Air Fried Lemon Pepper Shrimp

Ingredients

- Lemon - 1
- Lemon pepper - 1 teaspoon
- Olive oil - 1 tablespoon
- Garlic powder - 1/4 teaspoon
- Paprika - 1/4 teaspoon
- Deveined and peeled shrimps - 12 ounces
- Sliced lemon – 1

Method

1. Set the temperature of an air fryer to 200C.

2. Mix lemon pepper, garlic powder, and olive oil, paprika and lemon juice in a clean bowl. Coat shrimps by this mixture by tossing.

3. Put shrimps in an air fryer and cook for 5-8 minutes until its color turn to pink. Dish out cooked shrimps and serve with lemon slices.

24. Air Fried Shrimp a la Bang Bang

Ingredients

- Deveined raw shrimps - 1 pound
- Sweet chili sauce - 1/4 cup
- Plain flour - 1/4 cup
- Green onions - 2
- Mayonnaise - 1/2 cup
- Sriracha sauce - 1 tablespoon
- Bread crumbs - 1 cup
- Leaf lettuce - 1 head

Method

1. Set the temperature of an air fryer to 200C

2. Make a bang bang sauce by mixing chili sauce, mayonnaise and sriracha sauce in a clean bowl. Separate some sauce for dipping in a separate small bowl.

3. Place bread crumbs and flour in two different plates. Coat shrimps with mayonnaise mixture, then with flour and then bread crumbs. Set coated shrimps on a baking paper.

4. Place them in an air fryer pot and cook for 10-12 minutes. Repeat this step for the rest of shrimps. Transfer shrimps to a clean dish and serve with green onions and lettuce.

25. Air Fried Spicy Bay Scallops

Ingredients

- Bay scallops - 1 pound
- Chili powder - 2 teaspoons
- Smoked paprika- 2 teaspoons
- Garlic powder - 1 teaspoon
- Olive oil - 2 teaspoons
- Black pepper powder - 1/4 teaspoon
- Cayenne red pepper - 1/8 teaspoon

Method

1. Set the temperature of an air fryer to 200C

2. Mix smoked paprika, olive oil, bay scallops, garlic powder, pepper, chili powder and cayenne pepper in a clean bowl and stir properly. Shift this mixture to an air fryer.

3. Air fry for 6-8 minutes with constant shaking until scallops are fully cooked. Transfer this dish in a clean plate and serve immediately.

26. Air Fried Breakfast Fritatta

Ingredients

- Fully cooked breakfast sausages - 1/4 pound
- Cheddar Monterey Jack cheese - 1/2 cup
- Green onion - 1
- Cayenne pepper - 1 pinch
- Red bell pepper - 2 tablespoons
- Eggs - 4
- Cooking oil - to spray

Method

1. Set the temperature of an air fryer to 180C.

2. Mix eggs, sausages, Cheddar Monterey Jack cheese, onion, bell pepper and cayenne in a clean bowl and stir to mix properly.

3. Spray cooking oil on a clean non-stick cake pan. Put egg mixture in the cake pan. Air fry for 15-20 minutes until fritatta is fully cooked and set. Transfer it in a clean plate and serve immediately.

27. Air Fried Roasted Okra

Ingredients

- Trimmed and sliced Okra - 1/2 pound
- Black pepper powder - 1/8 teaspoon
- Olive oil - 1 teaspoon
- Salt - 1/4 teaspoon

Method

1. Set the temperature of an air fryer to 175C.

2. Mix olive oil, black pepper, salt and okra in a clean bowl and stir to mix properly.

3. Make a single layer of this mixture in an air fryer pot. Air fry for 5-8 minutes with constant stirring. Cook for more 5 minutes and again toss. Cook for more 3 minutes and dish out in a clean plate and serve immediately.

28. Air Fried Rib-Eye Steak

Ingredients

- Rib-eye steak - 2 (1 1/2 inch thick)
- Olive oil - 1/4 cup
- Grill seasoning - 4 teaspoons
- Reduced sodium soy sauce - 1/2 cup

Method

1. Mix olive oil, soy sauce, seasoning and steaks in a clean bowl and set aside meat for marination.

2. Take out steaks and waste the remaining mixture. Remove excess oil from steak by patting.

3. Add 1 tablespoon water in an air fryer pot for the prevention from smoking during cooking of steaks.

3. Set the temperature of an air fryer to 200C. Place steaks in an air fryer pot. Air fry for 7-8 minutes and turn its side after every 8 minutes. Cook for more 7 minutes until it is rarely medium. Cook for final 3 minutes for a medium steak and dish out in a clean plate and serve immediately.

29. Air Fried Potato Chips

Ingredients

- Large potatoes - 2
- Olive oil - to spray
- Fresh parsley - optional
- Sea salt - 1/2 teaspoon

Method

1. Set the temperature of an air fryer to 180C.

2. Peel off the potatoes and cut them into thin slices. Shift the slices in a bowl containing ice chilled water and soak for 10 minutes. Drain potatoes, again add chilled water and soak for more 15 minutes.

3. Remove water from potatoes and allow to dry by using paper towel. Spray potatoes with cooking oil and add salt according to taste.

4. Place a single layer of potatoes slices in an oiled air fryer pot and cook for 15-18 minutes until color turns to golden brown and crispy. Stir constantly and turn its sides after every 5 minutes.

5. Dish out these crispy chips and serve with parsley.

30. Air Fried Tofu

Ingredients

- Packed tofu - 14 ounces
- Olive oil - 1/4 cup
- Reduced sodium soy sauce - 3 tablespoons
- Crushed red pepper flakes - 1/4 teaspoon
- Green onions - 2
- Cumin powder - 1/4 teaspoon
- Garlic - 2 cloves

Method

1. Set the temperature of an air fryer to 200C.

2. Mix olive oil, soy sauce, onions, garlic, cumin powder and red pepper flakes in a deep bowl to make marinade mixture.

3. Cut 3/8 inches' thick slices of tofu lengthwise and then diagonally. Coat tofu with marinade mixture. Place them in refrigerate for 4-5 minutes and turn them after every 2 minutes.

4. Place tofu in buttered air fryer pot. Put remaining marinade over each tofu. Cook for 5-8 minutes until color turns to golden brown. Dish out cooked tofu and serve immediately.

31. Air Fried Acorn Squash Slices

Ingredients

- Medium sized acorn squash - 2
- Soft butter - 1/2 cup

- Brown sugar - 2/3 cup

Method

1. Set the temperature of an air fryer to 160C.

2. Cut squash into two halves from length side and remove seeds. Again cut these halves into half inch slices.

3. Place a single layer of squash on buttered air fryer pot. Cook each side of squash for 5 minutes.

4. Mix butter into brown sugar and spread this mixture on the top of every squash. Cook for more 3 minutes. Dish out and serve immediately.

32. Air Fried Red Potatoes

Ingredients

- Baby potatoes - 2 pounds
- Olive oil - 2 tablespoons

- Fresh rosemary - 1 tablespoon
- Garlic - 2 cloves
- Salt - 1/2 teaspoon
- Black pepper - 1/4 teaspoon

Method

1. Set the temperature of an air fryer to 198C.

2. Cut potatoes into wedges. Coat them properly with minced garlic, rosemary, black pepper and salt.

3. Place coated potatoes on buttered air fryer pot. Cook potatoes for 5 minutes until golden brown and soft. Stir them at once. Dish out in a clean plate and serve immediately.

33. Air Fried Butter Cake

Ingredients

- Melted butter - 7 tablespoons
- White sugar - 1/4 cup & 2 tablespoons
- Plain flour - 1 & 2/3 cup

- Egg - 1
- Salt - 1 pinch
- Milk - 6 tablespoons
- Cooking oil - to spray

Method

1. Set the temperature of an air fryer to 180C and spray with cooking oil.

2. Beat white sugar, and butter together in a clean bowl until creamy and light. Then add egg and beautiful fluffy and smooth. Add salt and flour and stir. Then add milk and mix until batter is smooth. Shift batter to an preheated air fryer pot and level its surface by using spatula.

3. Place in an air fryer and set time of 15 minutes. Bake and check cake after 15 minutes by inserting toothpick in the cake. If toothpick comes out clean it means cake has fully baked.

4. Take out cake from air fryer and allow it to cool for 5-10 minutes. Serve immediately and enjoy.

34. Air Fried Jelly and Peanut Butter S'mores

Ingredients

- Chocolate topping peanut butter cup - 1
- Raspberry jam (seedless) - 1 teaspoon
- Marshmallow - 1 large
- Chocolate cracker squares – 2

Method

1. Set the temperature of an air fryer to 200C.

2. Put peanut butter cup on one cracker square and topped with marshmallow and jelly. Carefully transfer it in the preheated air fryer.

3. Cook for 1 minute until marshmallow becomes soft and light brown. Remaining cracker squares is used for topping.

4. Shift this delicious in a clean plate and serve immediately.

35. Air Fried Sun-Dried Tomatoes

Ingredients

- Red grape tomatoes - 5 ounces
- Olive oil - 1/4 teaspoon
- Salt - to taste

Method

1. Set the temperature of an air fryer to 115C.

2. Combine tomatoes halves, salt and olive oil evenly in a clean bowl. Shift tomatoes in an air fryer pot by placing skin side down.

3. Cook in air fryer for 45 minutes. Smash tomatoes by using spatula and cook for more 30 minutes. Repeat this step with the rest of tomatoes.

4. Shift this delicious dish in a clean plate and allow it to stand for 45 minutes to set. Serve this dish and enjoy.

36. Air Fried Sweet Potatoes Tots

Ingredients:

- Peeled Sweet Potatoes - 2 small (14oz.total)
- Garlic Powder - 1/8 tsp
- Potato Starch - 1 tbsp
- Kosher Salt, Divided - 11/4 tsp
- Unsalted Ketchup - 3/4 Cup
- Cooking Oil for spray

Method:

1. Take water in a medium pan and give a single boil over high flame. Then, add the sweet potatoes in the boiled water & cook for 15 minutes till potatoes becomes soft. Move the potatoes to a cooling plate for 15 minutes.

2. Rub potatoes using the wide hole's grater over a dish. Apply the potato starch, salt and garlic powder and toss gently. Make almost 24 shaped cylinders (1-inch) from the mixture.

3. Coat the air fryer pot gently with cooking oil. Put single layer of 1/2 of the tots in the pot and spray with cooking oil. Cook at 400 °F for about 12 to 14 minutes till lightly browned and flip tots midway. Remove from the pot and sprinkle with salt. Repeat with rest of the tots and salt left over. Serve with ketchup immediately.

37. Air Fried Banana Bread

Ingredients:

- White Whole Wheat Flour - 3/4 cup (3 oz.)
- Mashed Ripe Bananas - 2 medium or (about 3/4th cup)
- Cinnamon powder– 4 pinches
- Kosher Salt - 1/2 tsp
- Baking Soda - 1/4 tsp
- Large Eggs, Lightly Beaten - 2
- Regular Sugar - 1/2 cup
- Vanilla Essence - 1 tsp
- Vegetable Oil - 2 tbsp
- Roughly Chopped and toasted Walnuts - 2 table-spoons (3/4 oz.)
- Plain Non-Fat Yogurt - 1/3 cup
- Cooking Oil for Spray - as required

Method:

1. Cover the base of a 6-inches round cake baking pan with baking paper and lightly brush with melted butter. Beat the flour, baking soda, salt, and cinnamon together in a clean bowl and let it reserve.

2. Whisk the mashed bananas, eggs, sugar, cream, oil and vanilla together in a separate bowl. Stir the wet ingredients gently into the flour mixture until everything is blended. Pour the mixture in the prepared pan and sprinkle with the walnuts.

3. Set the temperature of an air fryer to 310 °F and put the pan in the air fryer. Cook until browned, about 30 to 35 minutes. Rotate the pan periodically until a wooden stick put in it and appears clean. Before flipping out & slicing, move the bread to a cooling rack for 15 minutes.

38. Air Fried Avocado Fries

Ingredients:

- Avocados --. 2 - Cut each into the 8 pieces
- All-purpose flour - 1/2 cup (about 21/8 oz.)
- Panko (Japanese Style Breadcrumbs) - 1/2 cup
- Large Eggs - 2
- Kosher Salt - 1/4 tsp
- Apple Cider - 1 tbsp
- Sriracha Chilli Sause - 1 tbsp
- Black pepper - 11/2 tsp
- Water - 1 tbsp
- Unsalted Ketchup - 1/2 cup
- Cooking spray

Method:

1. Mix flour and pepper collectively in a clean bowl. Whip eggs & water gently in another bowl. Take panko in a third bowl. Coat avocado slices in flour and remove extra flour by shaking. Then, dip the slices in the egg and remove any excess. Coat in panko by pushing to stick together. Spray well the avocado slices with cooking oil.

2. In the air fryer's basket, put avocado slices & fry at 400 ° F until it turns into golden for 7-8 minutes. Turn avocado wedges periodically while frying. Take out from an air fryer and use salt for sprinkling.

3. Mix the Sriracha, ketchup, vinegar, and mayonnaise together in a small bowl. Put two tablespoons of sauce on each plate with 4 avocado fries before serving.

39. "Strawberry Pop Tarts" in an Air Fryer

Ingredients:

- Quartered Strawberries - (about 13/4 cups equal to 8 ounces)
- White/Regular Sugar - 1/4 cup
- Refrigerated Piecrusts - 1/2(14.1-oz)

- Powdered Sugar - 1/2 cup (about 2-oz)
- Fresh Lemon Juice - 11/2 tsp
- Rainbow Candy Sprinkles - 1 tbsp(about 1/2 ounce)
- Cooking Spray

Method:

1. Mix strawberries & white sugar and stay for 15 minutes with periodically stirring. Air fryer them for 10 minutes until glossy and reduced with constant stirring. Let it cool for 30 minutes.

2. Use the smooth floured surface to roll the pie crust and make 12-inches round shape. Cut the dough into 12 rectangles of (2 1/2- x 3-inch), re-rolling strips if necessary. Leaving a 1/2-inch boundary, add the spoon around 2 tea-spoons of strawberry mixture into the middle of 6 of dough rectangles. Brush the edges of the rectangles of the filled dough with water. Then, press the edges of rest dough rectangles with a fork to seal. Spray the tarts very well with cooking oil.

3. In an air fryer pot, put 3 tarts in a single layer and cook them at 350 ° F for 10 minutes till golden brown. With the rest of the tarts, repeat the process. Set aside for cooling for 30 minutes.

4. In a small cup, whip the powdered sugar & lemon juice together until it gets smooth. Glaze the spoon over the cooled tarts and sprinkle equally with candy.

40. Lighten up Empanadas in an Air Fryer

Ingredients:

- Lean Green Beef - 3 ounces
- Cremini Mushrooms - Chopped finely - 3 ounces
- White onion - Chopped finely - 1/4th cup
- Garlic – Chopped finely - 2 tsp.
- Pitted Green Olives - 6
- Olive Oil - 1 table-spoon
- Cumin - 1/4th tsp
- Cinnamon - 1/8th tsp
- Chopped tomatoes - 1/2 cup
- Paprika - 1/4 tea-spoon
- Large egg lightly Beaten - 1
- Square gyoza wrappers - 8

Method:

1. In a medium cooking pot, let heat oil on the medium/high temperature. Then, add beef & onion; for 3 minutes, cook them, mixing the crumble, until getting brown. Put the mushrooms; let them cook for 6 mins, till the mushrooms start to brown, stirring frequently. Add the paprika, olives, garlic, cinnamon, and cumin; cook for three minutes until the mushrooms are very tender and most of the liquid has been released. Mix in the tomatoes and cook, turning periodically, for 1 minute. Put the filling in a bowl and let it cool for 5 minutes.

2. Arrange 4 wrappers of gyoza on a worktop. In each wrapper, put around 1 1/2 tablespoons of filling in the middle. Clean the edges of the egg wrappers; fold over the wrappers and pinch the edges to seal. Repeat with the remaining wrappers and filling process.

3. Place the 4 empanadas in one single layer in an air-fryer basket and cook for 7 minutes at 400 °F until browned well. Repeat with the empanadas that remain.

41. Air Fried Calzones

Ingredients:

- Spinach Leaves --> 3 ounces (about 3 cups)
- Shredded Chicken breast --> 2 ounces (about 1/3 cup)
- Fresh Whole Wheat Pizza Dough --> 6 ounces
- Shredded Mozzarella Cheese --> 11/2 ounces (about 6 tbsp)
- Low Sodium Marinara Sauce --> 1/3 cup

Method:

1. First of all, in a medium pan, let heat oil on medium/high temperature. Include onion & cook, continue mixing then well efficiently, for two min, till get soft. After that, add the spinach; then cover & cook it until softened. After that, take out the pan from the heat; mix the chicken & marinara sauce.

2. Divide the dough in to the four identical sections. Then, roll each section into a 6-inches circle on a gently floured surface. Place over half of each dough circular shape with one-fourth of the spinach mixture. Top with one-fourth of the cheese each. Fold the dough to make half-moons and over filling, tightening the edges to lock. Coat the calzones well with spray for cooking

3. In the basket of an air fryer, put the calzones and cook them at 325 ° F until the dough becomes nicely golden brown, in 12 mins, changing the sides of the calzones after 8 mins.

42. Air Fried Mexican Style Corns

Ingredients:

- Unsalted Butter - 11/2 tbsp.
- Chopped Garlic -2 tsp
- Shucked Fresh Corns - 11/2 lb
- Fresh Chopped Cilantro - 2 tbsp.
- Lime zest - 1 tbsp.
- Lime Juice - 1 tsp
- Kosher Salt - 1/2 tsp
- Black Pepper - 1/2 tsp

Method:

1. Coat the corn delicately with the cooking spray, and put the corn in the air fryer's basket in one single layer. Let it Cooking for 14 mins at 400 °F till tender then charred gently, changing the corn half the way via cooking.

2. In the meantime, whisk together all the garlic, lime juice, butter, & lime zest in the microwaveable pot. Let an air fryer on Fast, about 30 seconds, until the butter melts and the garlic is aromatic. Put the corn on the plate and drop the butter mixture on it. Using the salt, cilantro, and pepper to sprinkle. Instantly serve this delicious recipe.

43. Air Fryer Crunchy & Crispy Chocolate Bites

Ingredients:

- Frozen Shortcrust Pastry - Partially thawed -- 4
- Cinnamon for dusting -- as required
- Icing Sugar for dusting -- as required
- Mars Celebration Chocolates -- 24
- Whipped Cream - as required

Method:

1. First of all, cut each pastry sheet into 6 equal rectangles. Brush the egg finely. In the centre of each piece of the pastry, place one chocolate. Fold the pastry over to seal the chocolate. Trim the extra pastry, then press and lock the corners. Put it on a tray lined with baking sheet. Brush the tops with an egg. Use the mixture of cinnamon and sugar to sprinkle liberally.

2. In the air-fryer basket, put a layer of the baking paper, ensuring that the paper is 1 cm smaller than that of the basket to permit air to circulate well. Place the 6 pockets in basket, taking care that these pockets must not to overlap. Then, cook them for 8-9 mins at 190 ° C till they become golden and the pastry are prepared thoroughly. As the pockets cooked, transfer them into a dish. Repeat the process with the pockets that remain.

3. After taking out from the air fryer, dust the Icing sugar and at last with whipped cream. Serve them warm.

44. Doritos-Crumbled Chicken tenders in an Air fryer

Ingredients:

- Buttermilk -- 1 cup (about 250ml)
- Doritos Nacho Cheese Corn Chips -- 170g Packet
- Halved Crossways Chicken Tenderloins -- 500g
- Egg -- 1
- Plain Flour -- 50g
- Mild Salsa -- for serving

Method:

1.Take a ceramic bowl or glass and put the chicken in it. Then, c over the buttermilk with it. Wrap it and put it for 4 hours or may be overnight in the refrigerator to marinate.

2. Let Preheat an air fryer at 180C. Then, cover a Baking tray with grease-proof paper.

3. In a Chopper, add the corn chips then pulse them until the corn chips become coarsely chopped. Then, transfer the chopped chips to a dish. In a deep cup, put the egg and beat it. On another plate, put the flour.

4. Remove the unnecessary water from the chicken, and also discard the buttermilk. Then, dip the chicken in the flour mixture and wipe off the extra flour. After that, dip in the beaten egg and then into the chips of corn, press it firmly to coat well. Transfer it to the tray that made ready to next step.

5. In the air fryer, put half of the chicken and then, fry for 8 to 10 mins until they are golden as well as cooked completely. Repeat the process with the chicken that remain.

Transfer the chicken in the serving dish. Enjoy this delicious recipe with salsa.

45. Air Fryer Ham & Cheese Croquettes

Ingredients:

- Chopped White Potatoes -- 1 kg
- Chopped Ham -- 100g
- Chopped Green Shallots -- 2
- Grated Cheddar Cheese -- 80g (about 1 cup)
- All-purpose flour -- 50g
- eggs -- 2
- Breadcrumbs -- 100g
- Lemon Slices -- for serving

- Tonkatsu Sause -- for serving

Method:

1. In a large-sized saucepan, put the potatoes. Cover with chill water. Carry it over high temperature to a boil. Boil till tender for 10 to 12 minutes. Drain thoroughly. Return over low heat to pan. Mix until it is smooth and has allowed to evaporate the certain water. Withdraw from the sun. Switch to a tub. Fully set aside to chill.

2. Then, add the shallot, Ham and cheese in the mashed potatoes also season with kosher salt. Mix it well. Take the 2 tablespoons of the mixture and make its balls. And repeat process for the rest of mixture.

3. Take the plain flour in a plate. Take another small bowl and beat the eggs. Take the third bowl and add the breadcrumbs in it. Toss the balls in the flour. Shake off the extra flour then in eggs and coat the breadcrumbs well. Make the balls ready for frying. Take all the coated balls in the fridge for about 15 minutes.

4. Preheat an air fryer at 200 ° C. Then, cook the croquettes for 8 to10 mints until they become nicely golden, in two rounds. Sprinkle the tonkatsu sauce and serve the croquettes with lemon slices.

46. Air Fryer Lemonade Scones

Ingredients:

- Self-raising flour -- 525g (about 3 1/2 cups)

- Thickened Cream -- 300ml

- Lemonade -- 185ml (about 3/4 cup)

- Caster Sugar -- 70g (1/3 cup)

- Vanilla Essence -- 1 tsp

- Milk -- for brushing

- Raspberry Jam -- for serving

- Whipped Cream -- for serving

Method:

1. In a large-sized bowl, add the flour and sugar together. Mix it well. Add lemonade, vanilla and cream. In a big bowl, add the flour and sugar. Just make a well. Remove milk, vanilla and lemonade. Mix finely, by using a plain knife, till the dough comes at once.

2. Take out the dough on the flat surface and sprinkle the dry flour on the dough. Knead it gently for about 30 secs until the dough get smooth. On a floured surface,

roll out the dough. Politely knead for thirty seconds, until it is just smooth. Form the dough into a round shape about 2.5 cm thick. Toss around 5.5 cm blade into the flour. Cut the scones out. Push the bits of remaining dough at once gently and repeat the process to make Sixteen scones.

3. In the air fryer bucket, put a layer of baking paper, ensuring that the paper is 1 cm shorter than the bucket to allow air to flow uniformly. Put 5 to 6 scones on paper in the bucket, even hitting them. Finely brush the surfaces with milk. Let cook them for about 15 mins at 160 ° C or when they tapped on the top, until become golden and empty-sounding. Move it safely to a wire or cooling rack. Repeat the same process with the rest of scones and milk two more times.

4. Serve the lemonade scones warm with raspberry jam & whipped cream.

47. Air Fryer Baked Potatoes

Ingredients:

- Baby Potatoes -- Halved shape -- 650g
- Fresh rosemary sprigs-- 2 large
- Sour Cream -- for serving
- Sweet Chilli Sauce -- for serving
- Salt -- for seasoning

Method:

1. Firstly, at 180C, pre-heat the air fryer. In an air fryer, put the rosemary sprigs & baby potatoes. Use oil for spray and salt for seasoning. Then, cook them for fifteen min until become crispy and cooked completely, also turning partially.

2. Serve the baked potatoes sweet chilli Sause & sour cream to enhance its flavour.

48. Air Fryer Mozzarella Chips

Ingredients:

- All-purpose flour -- 1 tbsp
- Breadcrumbs -- 2/3 cup
- Garlic Powder -- 3 tbsp
- Lemon Juice -- 1/3 cup
- Avocado -- 1
- Basil Pesto -- 2 tbsp
- Plain Yogurt -- 1/4 cup
- Chopped Green Onion --1
- Cornflakes crumbs -- 1/4 cup
- Mozzarella block -- 550g

- Eggs – 2
- Olive Oil for spray

Method:

1. Start making Creamy and fluffy Avocado Dipped Sauce: In a small-sized food processor, put the yogurt, avocado, lemon juice, onion, and pesto. Also add the pepper & salt, blend properly. Process it well until it get mixed and smooth. Switch the batter to a bowl. Cover it. Place in the fridge, until It required.

2. Take a large-sized tray and place a baking sheet.   In a large bowl, add the garlic powder & plain flour together. Also add the salt and season well. Take another medium bowl, whisk the eggs. Mix the breadcrumbs well in bowl.

3. Make the 2 cm thick wedges of mozzarella, then put them into the sticks. For coating, roll the cheese in the flour. Shake off the extra flour. Then, coat the sticks in the egg fusion, then in the breadcrumbs, operating in rounds. Place the prepared plate on it. Freeze till solid, or even for around 1 hour.

4. Spray the oil on the mozzarella lightly. Wrap the air fryer bucket with baking sheet, leaving an edge of 1 cm to enable air to flow. Then, cook at 180C, for 4 to 4 1/2 mins until the sticks become crispy & golden. Serve warm with sauce to dip.

49. Air Fryer Fetta Nuggets

Ingredients:

- All-purpose flour -- 1 tbsp.
- Chilli flakes -- 1 tsp
- Onion powder -- 1 tsp
- Sesame Seeds -- 1/4 cup
- Fetta Cheese Cubes -- Cut in 2 cm 180g
- Fresh Chives -- for serving
- Breadcrumbs -- 1/4 cup

BARBECUE SAUSE:

- apple cider -- 11/2 tsp
- Chilli Flakes -- 1/2 tsp
- Barbecue Sause -- 1//4 cup

Method:

1. Mix the onion powder, flour and chilli flakes in a medium-sized bowl. Use pepper for seasoning. Take another bowl, and beat an egg. Take one more bowl and mix sesame seeds and breadcrumbs. Then, toss the fetta in the chilli flakes,

onion powder & flour mixture. Dip the fetta in egg, and toss again in breadcrumbs fusion. Put them on a plate.

2. Pre- heat the air fryer at 180 °C. Put the cubes of fetta in a baking tray, in the basket of the air fryer. cook till fetta cubes become golden, or may be for 6 mins.

3. In the meantime, mix all the wet ingredients and create the Barbecue sauce.

4. Sprinkle the chives on the fetta and serve with Barbecue Sause.

50. Air Fryer Japanese Chicken Tender

Ingredients:

- McCormick Katsu Crumb for seasoning -- 25g
- Pickled Ginger -- 1 tbsp.
- Japanese-Style Mayonnaise -- 1/3 cup
- Chicken Tenderloins -- 500g
- Oil for spray

Method:

1. Put the chicken on tray in the form of single layer. Sprinkle the half seasoning on chicken. Then, turn chicken and sprinkle the seasoning again evenly. Use oil for spray on it.

2. Pre-heat at 180°C, an air fryer. Let the chicken cooking for about 12 - 14 mins until it becomes golden & cooked completely.

3. In the meantime, take a small-sized bowl, mix the mayonnaise and the remaining pickling sauce.

4. Serve the chicken with white sauce and put the ginger on the side, in a platter.

51. Whole-Wheat Pizzas in an Air Fryer

Ingredients:

- Low-sodium Marinara Sauce -- 1/4 cup
- Spinach leaves -- 1 cup
- Pita Breads -- 2
- Shredded Mozzarella Cheese -- 1/4 cup
- Parmigiano- Reggiano Cheese -- 1/4 ounces (about 1 tbsp.)
- Tomato slices -- 8
- Sliced Garlic Clove -- 1

Method:

1. Spread the marinara sauce on 1 side of each pita bread uniformly. Cover the cheese spinach leaves, tomato slices and garlic, with half of each of these.

2. Put one pita bread in an air fryer pot, then cook it at 350°F till the cheese becomes melted and pita becomes crispy, 4 - 5 mins. Repeat the process with the pita leftover.

52. Air Fryer Crispy Veggie Quesadillas

Ingredients:

* 6 inches Whole Grain Flour Tortillas -- 4
* Full fat Cheddar Cheese -- 4 ounces (about 1 cup)
* Sliced Zucchini -- 1 cup
* Lime Zest -- 1 tbsp.
* Lime Juice -- 1 tsp.
* Fresh Cilantro -- 2 tbsp.
* Chopped Red Bell Pepper -- (about 1 cup)
* Cumin -- 1/4 tsp.
* Low-fat Yoghurt -- 2 ounces
* Refrigerated Pico de Gallo -- 1/2 cup
* Oil for spray

Method:

1. Put tortillas on the surface of the work. Sprinkle onto half of each tortilla with 2 tbsp. of grated cheese. Cover each tortilla with 1/4 cup of chopped red bell pepper, zucchini chunks & the black beans on the top of the cheese. Sprinkle finely with 1/2 cup of cheese left. Fold over the tortillas to create quesadillas form like half-moons. Coat the quesadillas slightly with a cooking spray, & lock them with match picks or toothpicks.

2. Lightly brush a bucket of air fryer with cooking oil spray. Place 2 quesadillas carefully in the basket. Cook at 400°F till the tortillas become golden brown & gently crispy. Melt the cheese & gradually tender the vegetables for ten mins, tossing the quesadillas partially throughout the cooking period. Repeat the process with leftover quesadillas.

3. Mix together lime zest, yogurt, cumin, & lime juice, in a small-sized bowl since the quesadillas getting prepare. Break each quesadilla in-to the pieces to serve and then sprinkle the coriander.   With one tbsp. of cumin cream and two tablespoons of pico de gallo, and serve each.

53. Air Fried Curry Chickpeas

Ingredients:

- Drained & Rinsed Un-Salted Chickpeas -- 11/2 cups (15-oz.)
- Olive Oil -- 2 tbsp.
- Curry Powder -- 2 tsp.
- Coriander -- 1/4 tsp.
- Cumin -- 1/4 tsp.
- Cinnamon -- 1/4 tsp.
- Turmeric -- 1/2 tsp.
- Aleppo Pepper -- 1/2 tsp.
- Red Wine Vinegar -- 2 tbsp.
- Kosher Salt -- 1/4 tsp.
- Sliced Fresh Cilantro -- as required

Method:

1. Break the chickpeas lightly in a medium-sized bowl with your hands (don't crush them); and then remove the skins of chickpea.

2. Add oil & vinegar to the chickpeas, and stir to coat. Then, add curry powder, turmeric, coriander, cumin, & cinnamon; mix gently to combine them.

3. In the air fryer bucket, put the chickpeas in one single layer & cook at 400°F temperature until becoming crispy, for about 15 min, stirring the chickpeas periodically throughout the cooking process.

4. Place the chickpeas in a dish. Sprinkle the salt, cilantro and Aleppo pepper on chickpeas; and cover it.

54. Air Fried Beet Chips

Ingredients:

- Canola Oil -- 1 tsp.
- Medium-sized Red Beets -- 3
- Black Pepper -- 1/4 tsp.
- Kosher Salt -- 3/4 tsp.

Method:

1. Cut and Peel the red beets. Make sure each beet cutted into 1/8-inch-thick slices. Take a large-sized bowl and toss the beets slices, pepper, salt and oil well.

2. Put half beets in air fryer bucket and then cook at the 320°F temperature about 25 - 30 mins or until they become crispy and dry. Flip the bucket about every 5 mins. Repeat the process for the beets that remain.

55. Double-Glazed Air Fried Cinnamon Biscuits

Ingredients:

- Cinnamon -- 1/4 tsp.
- Plain Flour -- 2/3 cup (about 27/8 oz.)
- Whole-Wheat Flour -- 2/3 cup (about22/3 oz.)
- Baking Powder -- 1 tsp.
- White Sugar -- 2 tbsp.
- Kosher Salt -- 1/4 tsp.
- Chill Salted Butter -- 4 tbsp.
- Powdered Sugar -- 2 cups (about 8-oz.)
- Water -- 3 tbsp.
- Whole Milk -- 1/3 cup
- Oil for spray -- as required

Method:

1. In a medium-sized bowl, stir together salt, plain flour, baking powder, white sugar cinnamon and butter. Use two knives or pastry cutter to cut mixture till butter becomes well mixed with the flour and the mixture seems to as coarse cornmeal. Add the milk, then mix well until the dough becomes a ball. Place the dough on a floury surface and knead for around 30 seconds until the dough becomes smooth. Break the dough into 16 identical parts. Roll each part carefully into a plain ball.

2. Coat the air fryer pot well with oil spray. Put 8 balls in the pot, by leaving the space between each one; spray with cooking oil. Cook them until get browned & puffed, for 10 - 12 mins at 350°F temperature. Take out the doughnut balls from the pot carefully and put them on a cooling rack having foil for five mins. Repeat the process with the doughnut balls that remain.

3. In a medium pot, mix water and powdered sugar together until smooth. Then, spoon half of the glaze carefully over the doughnut balls. Cool for five mins and let it glaze once and enabling to drip off extra glaze.

56. Lemon Drizzle Cake in an Air Fryer

Ingredients:

- Grated Lemon rind -- 2 tsp.
- Cardamom -- 1 tsp.
- Softened Butter -- 150g
- Eggs -- 3
- Honey-flavoured Yoghurt -- 3/4 cup
- Self-raising flour -- 11/2 cups
- Caster Sugar -- 2/3 cup (150g)
- Lemon Zest -- for serving

LEMON ICING:

- Icing Sugar -- 1 cup
- Lemon Juice -- 11/2 tbsps.
- Softened Butter -- 10g

Method:

1. First, grease a 20 cm cake baking pan of round shape having butter paper. Take an electric beater and beat cardamom, sugar, lemon rind, and butter until the mixture becomes smooth & pale. Then, add the eggs one by one and beat well. Put the eggs in the flour and yoghurt. Fold by spatula and make the surface very smooth.

2. Pre-heat the air fryer at 180 C temperature. Put the pan in air fryer's pot. Bake it for about 35 mins. Check it by putting skewer in it that comes out clean without any sticky batter. Reserve it in the pan for 5 minutes to become cool before shifting it to a cooling rack.

3. Make the lemon glaze, add butter and icing sugar in a bowl. By adding lemon juice as required and form a smooth paste.

4. Put the cake on a plate to serve. Sprinkle the lemon zest and lemon icing to serve.

57. Air Fryer dukkah-Crumbed chicken

Ingredients:

- Chicken Thigh Fillets -- 8
- Herb or dukkah -- 45g packet

- Plain Flour -- 1/3 cup (about 50g)
- Kaleslaw kit -- 350g Packet
- Breadcrumbs -- 1 cup (about 80g)
- Eggs -- 2

Method:

1. Put half of the chicken within 2 sheets of cling paper. Gently beat until it remains 2 cm thick by using a meat hammer or rolling pin. Repeat the process with the chicken that remains.

2. In a deep bowl, mix breadcrumbs and dukkah together. Beat an egg in medium bowl., Put the flour and all the seasoning on a tray. Coat chicken pieces one by one in the flour and shake off the extra. Dip chicken pieces into the egg, then in breadcrumbs for coating. Move them to a dish. Cover them with the plastic wrapper & leave it to marinate for 30 mins in the fridge.

3. Pre-heat air fryer at 200°C temperature. Use olive oil to spray the chicken pieces. Put half of the chicken in one single layer in the air fryer pot. Cook them for about 16 mins and turning partially until they become golden & get cooked completely. Move to a plate & wrap them with foil to stay warm. Repeat the process with the chicken pieces that remains.

4. After that, place the kaleslaw kit in a serving bowl by following instructions mentioned in the packets.

5. Divide the prepared chicken & the kaleslaw between serving platters, and season it.

58. Air Fryer Vietnamese-style spring roll salad

Ingredients:

- Rice Noodles -- 340g
- Crushed Garlic -- 1 clove
- Grated Ginger -- 2 tsp.
- Pork Mince -- 250g
- Lemongrass paste -- 1 tsp
- Cutted into matchsticks the Peeled Carrots -- 2
- Sliced Spring onion -- 3
- Fish sauce -- 2 tsp.
- Spring roll pastries -- 10 sheets
- Coriander -- 1/2 cup
- Sliced Red Chilli - 1 long
- Vietnamese-style Salad -- for dressing
- Mint Leaves -- 1/2
- Bean Sprouts -- 1 cup

Method:

1. Take a large-sized saucepan and cook the noodles for about 4 mins until get soft. Take the cold water and discharge thoroughly. Cutting 1 cup of the boiled noodles into the short lengths, with the leftover noodles reserved.

2. Take a large-sized bowl, add the mince, lemongrass, ginger, garlic, half carrot, spring onion, and fish sauce together and mix them well.

3. On a clean surface, put one pastry paper. Add two tablespoons across 1 side of the mince fusion diagonally. With just a little spray, brush its opposite side. Fold and roll on the sides to completely cover the mince filling. Repeat the process with the sheets of pastry and fill the thin layer of mince mixture, that remain.

4. Pre-heat at 200°C, an air fryer. Use olive oil, spray on the spring rolls. Put in the bucket of air fryer and cook the spring rolls for fifteen mins until cooked completely. Change the sides half-way during cooking.

5. After that, equally split reserved noodles in the serving bowls. Place coriander, bean sprouts, mint and the remaining spring onion and carrots at the top of the serving bowl.

6. Then, break the spring rolls in the half and place them over the mixture of noodles. Sprinkle the chili and serve with Vietnamese-style salad dressing according to your taste.

59. Air Fryer Pizza Pockets

Ingredients:

- Olive oil - 2 tsp.
- Sliced Mushrooms - 6 (about 100g)
- Chopped Leg Ham - 50g
- Crumbled Fetta - 80g
- White Wraps - 4
- Basil Leaves - 1/4 cup
- Baby Spinach - 120g
- Tomato Paste - 1/3 cup
- Chopped Red Capsicum - 1/2
- Dried Oregano - 1/2 tsp
- Olive oil - for spray
- Green Salad - for serving

Method:

1. Heat oil on medium temperature in an air fryer. Cook capsicum for about five minutes until it starts to soften. Add mushrooms and cook them for another five mins until mushrooms become golden and evaporating any water left in the pan. Move mushrooms to another bowl. Leave them to cool for 10 mins.

2. Take a heatproof bowl and put spinach in it. Cover it with boiling water. Wait for 1 min until slightly wilted. Drain water and leave it to cool for about 10 mins.

3. Excessive spinach moisture is squeezed and applied to the capsicum mixture. Add the oregano, basil, ham and fetta. Season it with both salt & pepper. Mix it well to combine properly.

4. Put one wrapper on the smooth surface. Add 1 tbsp of tomato paste to the middle of the wrap. Cover it with a combination of 1-quarter of the capsicum. Roll up the wrap to completely enclose the filling, give it as the shape of parcel and folding the sides. To build four parcels, repeat the procedure with the remaining wraps, mixture of capsicum & tomato paste. Use oil spray on the tops.

5. Pre-heat the air fryer at 180 C temperature. Cook the parcels for 6 - 8 mins until they become golden & crispy, take out them and move to 2 more batches. Serve along with the salad.

60. Air Fryer Popcorn Fetta with Maple Hot Sauce

Ingredients:

- Marinated Fetta cubes - 265g
- Cajun for seasoning - 2 tsp.
- Breadcrumbs - 2/3 cups
- Corn flour - 2 tbsp.
- Egg - 1
- Chopped Fresh Coriander - 1 tbsp.

- Coriander leaves - for serving

Maple hot sauce:

- Maple syrup - 2 tbsp.
- Sriracha - 1 tbsps.

Method:

1. Drain the fetta, then reserve 1 tbsp of oil making sauce.

2. Take a bowl, mix the cornflour and the Cajun seasoning together. Beat the egg in another bowl. Take one more bowl and combine the breadcrumbs & cilantro in it. Season it with salt & pepper. Work in batches, coat the fetta in cornflour mixture, then dip in the egg. After that, toss them in breadcrumb mixture for coating. Place them on the plate and freeze them for one hour.

3. Take a saucepan, add Sriracha, reserved oil and maple syrup together and put on medium low heat. Stir it for 3 - 4 minutes continuously until sauce get start to thicken. Then, remove the maple sauce from heat.

4. Pre-heat the air fryer at 180C. Place the cubes of fetta in a single layer in the air fryer's pot. Cook them for 3 - 4 mins until just staring softened, and fettas

become golden. Sprinkled with extra coriander leaves and serve them with the maple hot sauce.

61. Air fryer Steak Fajitas

Ingredients:

- Chopped tomatoes - 2 large
- Minced Jalapeno pepper - 1
- Cumin - 2 tsp.
- Lime juice - 1/4 cup
- Fresh minced Cilantro - 3 tbsp.
- Diced Red Onion - 1/2 cup
- 8-inches long Whole-wheat tortillas - 6
- Large onion - 1 sliced
- Salt - 3/4 tsp divided
- Beef steak - 1

Method:

1. Mix first 5 ingredients in a clean bowl then stir in cumin and salt. Let it stand till before you serve.

2. Pre-heat the air fryer at 400 degrees. Sprinkle the cumin and salt with the steak that remain. Place them on buttered air-fryer pot and cook the steak until the meat reaches the appropriate thickness (a thermometer should read 135 ° for medium-rare; 140 °; moderate, 145 °), for 6 to 8 mins per side. Remove from the air fryer and leave for five min to stand.

3. Then, put the onion in the air-fryer pot. Cook it until get crispy-tender, stirring once for 2 - 3 mins. Thinly slice the steak and serve with onion & salsa in the tortillas. Serve it with avocado & lime slices if needed.

62. Air-Fryer Fajita-Stuffed Chicken

Ingredients:

- Boneless Chicken breast - 4
- Finely Sliced Onion - 1 small
- Finely Sliced Green pepper - 1/2 medium-sized
- Olive oil - 1 tbsp.
- Salt - 1/2 tsp.
- Chilli Powder - 1 tbsp.
- Cheddar Cheese - 4 ounces
- Cumin - 1 tsp.
- Salsa or jalapeno slices - optional

Method:

1. Pre-heat the air fryer at the 375 degrees. In the widest part of every chicken breast, cut a gap horizontally. Fill it with green pepper and onion. Combine olive oil and the seasonings in a clean bowl and apply over the chicken.

2. Place the chicken on a greased dish in the form of batches in an air-fryer pot. Cook it for 6 minutes. Stuff the chicken with cheese slices and secure the chicken pieces with toothpicks. Cook at 165° until for 6 to 8 minutes. Take off the toothpicks. Serve the delicious chicken with toppings of your choosing, if wanted.

63. Nashvilla Hot Chicken in an Air Fryer

Ingredients:

- Chicken Tenderloins - 2 pounds
- Plain flour - 1 cup
- Hot pepper Sauce - 2 tbsp.
- Egg - 1 large
- Salt - 1 tsp.
- Pepper - 1/2 tsp.
- Buttermilk - 1/2 cup
- Cayenne Pepper - 2 tbsp.
- Chilli powder - 1 tsp.
- Pickle Juice - 2 tbsp.
- Garlic Powder - 1/2 tsp.
- Paprika - 1 tsp.
- Brown Sugar - 2 tbsp.
- Olive oil - 1/2 cup
- Cooling oil for spray

Method:

1. Combine pickle juice, hot sauce and salt in a clean bowl and coat the chicken on its both sides. Put it in the fridge, cover it, for a minimum 1 hour. Throwing away some marinade.

2. Pre-heat the air fryer at 375 degrees. Mix the flour, the remaining salt and the pepper in another bowl. Whisk together the buttermilk, eggs, pickle juice and hot sauce well. For coating the both sides, dip the chicken in plain flour; drip off the excess. Dip chicken in egg mixture and then again dip in flour mixture.

3. Arrange the single layer of chicken on a greased air-fryer pot and spray with cooking oil. Cook for 5 to 6 minutes until it becomes golden brown. Turn and spray well. Again, cook it until golden brown, for more 5-6 minutes.

4. Mix oil, brown sugar, cayenne pepper and seasonings together. Then, pour on the hot chicken and toss to cover. Serve the hot chicken with pickles.

64. Southern-style Chicken

Ingredients:

- Crushed Crackers - 2 cups (about 50)
- Fresh minced parsley - 1 tbsp.
- Paprika - 1 tsp.
- Pepper - 1/2 tsp.
- Garlic salt - 1 tsp.
- Fryer Chicken - 1
- Cumin - 1/4 tsp.
- Egg - 1
- Cooking Oil for spray

Method:

1. Set the temperature of an air fryer at 375 degrees. Mix the first 7 ingredients in a deep bowl. Beat an egg in deep bowl. Soak the chicken in egg, then pat in the cracker mixture for proper coat. Place the chicken in a single layer on the greased air-fryer pot and spray with cooking oil.

2. Cook it for 10 minutes. Change the sides of chicken and squirt with cooking oil spray. Cook until the chicken becomes golden brown & juices seem to be clear, for 10 - 20 minutes longer.

65. Chicken Parmesan in an Air Fryer

Ingredients:

- Breadcrumbs - 1/2 cup
- Pepper - 1/4 tsp.
- Pasta Sauce - 1 cup
- Boneless Chicken breast - 4
- Mozzarella Cheese - 1 cup
- Parmesan Cheese - 1/3 cup
- Large Eggs - 2
- Fresh basil - Optional

Method:

1. Set the temperature of an air-fryer at 375 degrees. In a deep bowl, beat the eggs gently. Combine the breadcrumbs, pepper and parmesan cheese in another bowl. Dip the chicken in beaten egg and coat the chicken parmesan with breadcrumbs mixture.

2. In an air-fryer pot, put the chicken in single layer. Cook the chicken for 10 to 12 mins with changing the sides partially. Cover the chicken with cheese and sauce. Cook it for 3 to 4 minutes until cheese has melted. Then, sprinkle with basil leaves and serve.

66. Lemon Chicken Thigh in an Air Fryer

Ingredients:

- Bone-in Chicken thighs- 4
- Pepper - 1/8 tsp.
- Salt - 1/8 tsp.
- Pasta Sauce - 1 cup
- Lemon Juice - 1 tbsp.
- Lemon Zest - 1 tsp.
- Minced Garlic - 3 cloves

- Butter - 1/4 cup
- Dried or Fresh Rosemary - 1 tsp.
- Dried or Fresh Thyme - 1/4 tsp.

Method:

1. Pre-heat the air fryer at 400 degrees. Combine the butter, thyme, rosemary, garlic, lemon juice & zest in a clean bowl. Spread a mixture on each of the thigh's skin. Use salt and pepper to sprinkle.

2. Place the chicken, then side up the skin, in a greased air-fryer pot. Cook for 20 mins and flip once. Switch the chicken again (side up the skin) and cook it for about 5 mins until the thermometer will read 170 degrees to 175 degrees. Then, place in the serving plate and serve it.

67. Salmon with Maple-Dijon Glaze in air fryer

Ingredients:

- Salmon Fillets - 4 (about ounces)
- Salt - 1/4 tsp.
- Pepper - 1/4 tsp.
- Butter - 3 tbsp.

- Mustard - 1 tbsp.
- Lemon Juice - 1 medium-sized
- Garlic clove - 1 minced
- Olive oil

Method:

1. Pre-heat the air fryer at 400 degrees. Melt butter in a medium-sized pan on medium temperature. Put the mustard, minced garlic, maple syrup & lemon juice. Lower the heat and cook for 2 - 3 minutes before the mixture thickens significantly. Take off from the heat and set aside for few mins.

2. Brush the salmon with olive oil and also sprinkle the salt and pepper on it.

3. In an air fryer bucket, put the fish in a single baking sheet. Cook for 5 to 7 mins until fish is browned and easy to flake rapidly with help of fork. Sprinkle before to serve the salmon with sauce.

68. Air Fryer Roasted Beans

Ingredients:

- Fresh Sliced Mushrooms - 1/2 pounds
- Green Beans cut into 2-inch wedges - 1 pound
- Italian Seasoning - 1 tsp.

- Pepper - 1/8 tsp.
- Salt - 1/4 tsp.
- Red onion - 1 small
- Olive oil - 2 tbsp.

Method:

1. Pre-heat the air fryer at 375 degrees. Merge all of the ingredients in the large-sized bowl by tossing.

2. Assemble the vegetables on the greased air-fryer pot. Cook for 8 -10 minutes until become tender. Redistribute by tossing and cook for 8-10 minutes until they get browned.

69. Air Fried Radishes

Ingredients:

- Quartered Radishes - (about 6 cups)
- Fresh Oregano - 1 tbsp.

- Dried Oregano - 1 tbsp.
- Pepper - 1/8 tsp.
- Salt - 1/4 tsp.
- Olive Oil - 3 tbsp.

Method:

1. Set the temperature of an air fryer to 375 degrees. Mix the rest of the ingredients with radishes. In an air-fryer pot, put the radishes on greased dish.

2. Cook them for 12-15 minutes until they become crispy & tender with periodically stirring. Take out from the air fryer and serve the radishes in a clean dish.

70. Air Fried Catfish Nuggets

Ingredients

- Catfish fillets (1 inch) - 1 pound
- Seasoned fish fry coating - 3/4 cup
- Cooking oil - to spray

Method

1. Set the temperature of an air fryer to 200C.

2. Coat catfish pieces with seasoned coating mix by proper mixing from all sides.

3. Place nuggets evenly in an oiled air fryer pot. Spray both sides of nuggets with cooking oil. You can work in batches if the size of your air fryer is small.

4. Air fry nuggets for 5-8 minutes. Change sides of nuggets with the help of tongs and cook for more 5 minutes. Shift these delicious nuggets in a clean plate and serve immediately.

CONCLUSION:

This manual served you the easiest, quick, healthy and delicious foods that are made in an air fryer. It is also very necessary to cook food easily and timely without getting so much tired. We've discussed all the 70 easy, short, quick, delicious and healthy foods and dishes. These recipes can be made within few minutes. This manual provides the handiest or helpful cooking recipes for the busy people who are performing their routine tasks. Instead of ordering the costly or unhealthy food from hotels, you will be able to   make the easy, tasty and healthy dishes with minimum cost. By reading this the most informative handbook, you can learn, experience or make lots of recipes in an air with great taste because cooking food traditionally on the stove is quite difficult for the professional persons. With the help of an air fryer, you can make various dishes for a single person as well as the entire family timely and effortlessly. We conclude that this cook book will maintain your health and it would also be the source of enjoying dishes without doing great effort in less and budget.

Air Fryer Cookbook for Two

Cook and Taste Tens of Healthy Fried Recipes with Your Sweetheart. Burn Fat, Kill Hunger, and Improve Your Mood

By

Michelle Polpetta

Table of Contents

Introduction:

You have got the set of important knives, toaster oven, coffee machine, and quick pot along with the cutter you want to good care of. There may be a variety of things inside your kitchen, but maybe you wish to make more space for an air fryer. It's easy to crowd and load with the new cooking equipment even though you've a lot of them. However, an air fryer is something you will want to make space for.

The air fryer is identical to the oven in the way that it roasts and bakes, but the distinction is that elements of hating are placed over the top& are supported by a big, strong fan, producing food that is extremely crispy and, most importantly with little oil in comparison to the counterparts which are deeply fried. Usually, air fryers heat up pretty fast and, because of the centralized heat source & the fan size and placement, they prepare meals quickly & uniformly. The cleanup is another huge component of the air frying. Many baskets & racks for air fryers are dishwasher protected. We recommend a decent dish brush for those who are not dishwasher secure. It will go through all the crannies and nooks that facilitate the movement of air without making you crazy.

We have seen many rave reviews of this new trend, air frying. Since air frying, they argue, calls for fast and nutritious foods. But is the hype worth it? How do the air fryers work? Does it really fry food?

How do air fryers work?

First, let's consider how air fryer really works before we go to which type of air fryer is decent or any simple recipes. Just think of it; cooking stuff without oil is such a miracle. Then, how could this even be possible? Let's try to find out how to pick the best air fryer for your use now when you understand how the air fryer works.

How to pick the best air fryer

It is common to get lost when purchasing gadgets & electrical equipment, given that there're a wide range of choices available on the market. So, before investing in one, it is really ideal to have in mind the specifications and budget.

Before purchasing the air fryer, you can see the things you should consider:

Capacity/size: Air fryers are of various sizes, from one liter to sixteen liters. A three-liter capacity is fine enough for bachelors. Choose an air fryer that has a range of 4–6 liters for a family having two children. There is a restricted size of the basket which is used to put the food. You will have to prepare the meals in batches if you probably wind up using a tiny air fryer.

Timer: Standard air fryers arrive with a range timer of 30 minutes. For house cooking, it is satisfactory. Thought, if you are trying complex recipes which take a longer cooking time, pick the air fryer with a 1-hour timer.

Temperature: The optimum temperature for most common air fryers is 200 degrees C (400 f). You can quickly prepare meat dishes such as fried chicken, tandoori, kebabs etc.

The design, durability, brand value and controls are other considerations you might consider.

Now that you know which air fryer is best for you let's see the advantages of having an air fryer at your place.

What are the benefits of air fryers?

The benefits of air fryers are as follows:

Cooking with lower fat & will promote weight loss

Air fryers work with no oils and contain up to 80 percent lower fat than most fryers relative to a traditional deep fryer. Shifting to an air fryer may encourage loss of weight by decreasing fat & caloric intake for anyone who consumes fried food regularly and also has a problem with leaving the fast foods.

Faster time for cooking

Air frying is easier comparing with other cooking techniques, such as grilling or baking. Few air fryers need a preheat of 60 seconds, but others do not need a preheat any longer than a grill or an oven. So if there is a greater capacity or multiple compartments for the air fryer basket, you may make various dishes in one go.

Quick to clean

It's extremely easy to clean an air fryer. And after each use, air frying usually does not create enough of a mess except you cook fatty food such as steak or chicken wings. Take the air fryer out and clean it with soap & water in order to disinfect the air fryer.

Safer to be used

The air fryer is having no drawbacks, unlike hot plates or deep frying. Air fryers get hot, but splashing or spilling is not a risk.

Minimum use of electricity and environment friendly

Air fryers consume far less electricity than various electric ovens, saving your money & reducing carbon output.

Flexibility

Some of the air fryers are multi-functional. It's possible to heat, roast, steam, broil, fry or grill food.

Less waste and mess

Pan-fries or deep fryer strategies leave one with excess cooking oil, which is difficult to rid of and usually unsustainable. You can cook fully oil-less food with an air fryer. All the pieces have a coating of nonstick, dishwasher safe and nonstick coating.

Cooking without the use of hands

The air fryer includes a timer, & when it is full, it'll stop by itself so that you may feel secure while multitasking.

Feasible to use

It is very much convenient; you can use an air fryer whenever you want to. Few air fryers involve preheating, which is less than 5 minutes; with the air fryer, one may begin cooking immediately.

Reducing the possibility of the development of toxic acrylamide

Compared to making food in oil, air frying will decrease the potential of producing acrylamides. Acrylamide is a compound that, under elevated temperature cooking, appears in certain food and may have health impacts.

Chapter 1: Air fryer breakfast recipes

1. Air fryer breakfast frittata

Cook time: 20 minutes

Servings: 2 people

Difficulty: Easy

Ingredients:

- 1 pinch of cayenne pepper (not necessary)

- 1 chopped green onion

- Cooking spray

- 2 tbsp. diced red bell pepper

- ¼ pound fully cooked and crumbled breakfast sausages

- 4 lightly beaten eggs

- ½ cup shredded cheddar-Monterey jack cheese blend

Instructions:

1. Combine eggs, bell pepper, cheddar Monterey Jack cheese, sausages, cayenne and onion inside a bowl & blend to combine.

2. The air fryer should be preheated to 360 ° f (180° c). Spray a 6 by 2-inch non-stick cake pan along with a spray used in cooking.

3. Place the mixture of egg in the ready-made cake tray.

4. Cook for 18 - 20 minutes in your air fryer before the frittata is ready.

2. Air fryer banana bread

Cook time: 28 minutes

Serving: 8 people

Difficulty: Easy

Ingredients:

- 3/4 cup flour for all purposes

- 1/4 tbsp. salt

- 1 egg

- 2 mashed bananas overripe

- 1/4 cup sour cream

- 1/2 cup sugar

- 1/4 tbsp. baking soda

- 7-inch bundt pan

- 1/4 cup vegetable oil

- 1/2 tbsp. vanilla

Instructions:

1. In one tub, combine the dry ingredients and the wet ones in another. Mix the two slowly till flour is fully integrated, don't over mix.

2. With an anti-stick spray, spray and on a 7-inch bundt pan & then pour in the bowl.

3. Put it inside the air fryer basket & close. Placed it for 28 mins to 310 degrees

4. Remove when completed & permit to rest in the pan for about 5 mins.

5. When completed, detach and allow 5 minutes to sit in the pan. Then flip on a plate gently. Sprinkle melted icing on top, serve after slicing.

3. Easy air fryer omelet

Cook time: 8 minutes

Serving: 2 people

Difficulty: Easy

Ingredients:

- 1/4 cup shredded cheese

- 2 eggs

- Pinch of salt

- 1 teaspoon of McCormick morning breakfast seasoning – garden herb

- Fresh meat & veggies, diced

- 1/4 cup milk

Instructions:

1. In a tiny tub, mix the milk and eggs till all of them are well mixed.

2. Add a little salt in the mixture of an egg.

3. Then, in the mixture of egg, add the veggies.

4. Pour the mixture of egg in a greased pan of 6 by 3 inches.

5. Place your pan inside the air fryer container.

6. Cook for about 8 to 10 mins and at 350 f.

7. While you are cooking, slather the breakfast seasoning over the eggs & slather the cheese on the top.

8. With a thin spoon, loose the omelet from the pan and pass it to a tray.

9. Loosen the omelet from the sides of the pan with a thin spatula and pass it to a tray.

10. Its options to garnish it with additional green onions.

4. Air-fried breakfast bombs

Cook time: 20 mins

Serving: 2

Difficulty: easy

Ingredients:

- Cooking spray

- 1 tbsp. fresh chives chopped

- 3 lightly beaten, large eggs

- 4 ounces whole-wheat pizza dough freshly prepared

- 3 bacon slices center-cut

- 1 ounce 1/3-less-fat softened cream cheese

Instructions:

1. Cook the bacon in a standard size skillet for around 10 minutes, medium to very crisp. Take the bacon out of the pan; scatter. Add the eggs to the bacon drippings inside the pan; then cook, stirring constantly, around 1 minute, until almost firm and yet loose. Place the eggs in a bowl; add the cream cheese, the chives, and the crumbled bacon.

2. Divide the dough into four identical sections. Roll each bit into a five-inch circle on a thinly floured surface. Place a quarter of the egg mixture in the middle of each circle of dough. Clean the underside of the dough with the help of water; wrap the dough all around the mixture of an egg to form a purse and pinch the dough.

3. Put dough purses inside the air fryer basket in one layer; coat really well with the help of cooking spray. Cook for 5 to 6 minutes at 350 degrees f till it turns to a golden brown; check after 4 mins.

5. Air fryer French toast

Cook time: 15 mins

Serving: 2 people

Difficulty: easy

Ingredients:

- 4 beaten eggs

- 4 slices of bread

- Cooking spray (non-stick)

Instructions:

1. Put the eggs inside a container or a bowl which is sufficient and big, so the pieces of bread will fit inside.

2. With a fork, mix the eggs and after that, place each bread slice over the mixture of an egg.

3. Turn the bread for one time so that every side is filled with a mixture of an egg.

4. After that, fold a big sheet of aluminum foil; this will keep the bread together. Switch the foil's side; this will ensure that the mixture of an egg may not get dry. Now put the foil basket in the air fryer basket. Make sure to allow space around the edges; this will let the circulation of hot air.

5. With the help of cooking spray, spray the surface of the foil basket and then put the bread over it. On top, you may add the excess mixture of an egg.

6. For 5 mins, place the time to 365 degrees f.

7. Turn the bread & cook it again for about 3 to 5 mins, until it's golden brown over the top of the French toast & the egg isn't runny.

8. Serve it hot, with toppings of your choice.

6. Breakfast potatoes in the air fryer

Cook time: 15 mins

Servings: 2

Difficulty: easy

Ingredients:

• 1/2 tbsp. kosher salt

• 1/2 tbsp. garlic powder

• Breakfast potato seasoning

• 1/2 tbsp. smoked paprika

• 1 tbsp. oil

• 5 potatoes medium-sized. Peeled & cut to one-inch cubes (Yukon gold works best)

• 1/4 tbsp. black ground pepper

Instructions:

1. At 400 degrees f, preheat the air fryer for around 2 to 3 minutes. Doing this will provide you the potatoes that are crispiest.

2. Besides that, brush your potatoes with oil and breakfast potato seasoning till it is fully coated.

3. Using a spray that's non-stick, spray on the air fryer. Add potatoes & cook for about 15 mins, shaking and stopping the basket for 2 to 3 times so that you can have better cooking.

4. Place it on a plate & serve it immediately.

7. Air fryer breakfast pockets

Cook time: 15 mins

Serving: 5 people

Difficulty: easy

Ingredients:

- 2-gallon zip lock bags

- Salt & pepper to taste

- 1/3 + 1/4 cup of whole milk

- 1 whole egg for egg wash

- Cooking spray

- 1-2 ounces of Velveeta cheese

- Parchment paper

- 1 lb. of ground pork

- 2 packages of Pillsbury pie crust

- 2 crusts to a package

- 4 whole eggs

Instructions:

1. Let the pie crusts out of the freezer.

2. Brown the pig and rinse it.

3. In a tiny pot, heat 1/4 cup of cheese and milk until it is melted.

4. Whisk four eggs, season with pepper and salt & add the rest of the milk.

5. Fumble the eggs in the pan until they are nearly fully cooked.

6. Mix the eggs, cheese and meat together.

7. Roll out the pie crust & cut it into a circle of about 3 to 4 inches (cereal bowl size).

8. Whisk 1 egg for making an egg wash.

9. Put around 2 tbsp. of the blend in the center of every circle.

10. Now, eggs wash the sides of the circle.

11. Create a moon shape by folding the circle.

12. With the help of a fork, folded edges must be crimped

13. Place the pockets inside parchment paper & put it inside a ziplock plastic bag overnight.

14. Preheat the air fryer for 360 degrees until it is ready to serve.

15. With a cooking spray, each pocket side must be sprayed.

16. Put pockets inside the preheated air fryer for around 15 mins or till they are golden brown.

17. Take it out from the air fryer & make sure it's cool before you serve it.

8. Air fryer sausage breakfast casserole

Cook time: 20 mins

Serving: 6 people

Difficulty: easy

Ingredients:

- 1 diced red bell pepper

- 1 lb. ground breakfast sausage

- 4 eggs

- 1 diced green bell pepper

- 1/4 cup diced sweet onion

- 1 diced yellow bell pepper

- 1 lb. hash browns

Instructions:

1. Foil line your air fryer's basket.

2. At the bottom, put some hash browns.

3. Cover it with the raw sausage.

4. Place the onions & peppers uniformly on top.

5. Cook for 10 mins at 355 degrees.

6. Open your air fryer & blend the casserole a little if necessary.

7. Break every egg inside the bowl and spill it directly over the casserole.

8. Cook for the next 10 minutes for 355 degrees.

9. Serve with pepper and salt for taste.

9. Breakfast egg rolls

Cook time: 15 mins

Servings: 6 people

Difficulty: easy

Ingredients:

• Black pepper, to taste

- 6 large eggs

- Olive oil spray

- 2 tbsp. chopped green onions

- 1 tablespoon water

- 1/4 teaspoon kosher salt

- 2 tablespoons diced red bell pepper

- 1/2 pound turkey or chicken sausage

- 12 egg roll wrappers

- The salsa that is optional for dipping

Instructions:

1. Combine the water, salt and black pepper with the eggs.

2. Cook sausage in a non-stick skillet of medium size, make sure to let it cook in medium heat till there's no pink color left for 4 minutes, splitting into crumbles, then drain.

3. Stir in peppers and scallions & cook it for 2 minutes. Put it on a plate.

4. Over moderate flame, heat your skillet & spray it with oil.

5. Pour the egg mixture & cook stirring till the eggs are cooked and fluffy. Mix the sausage mixture.

6. Put one wrapped egg roll on a dry, clean work surface having corners aligned like it's a diamond.

7. Include an egg mixture of 1/4 cup on the lower third of your wrapper.

8. Gently raise the lower point closest to you & tie it around your filling.

9. Fold the right & left corners towards the middle & continue rolling into the compact cylinder.

10. Do this again with the leftover wrappers and fillings.

11. Spray oil on every side of your egg roll & rub it with hands to cover them evenly.

12. The air fryer must be preheated to 370 degrees f.

13. Cook the egg rolls for about 10 minutes in batches till it's crispy and golden brown.

14. Serve instantly with salsa, if required.

10. Air fryer breakfast casserole

Cook time: 45 mins

Servings: 6 people

Difficulty: medium

Ingredients:

- 1 tbsp. extra virgin olive oil

- Salt and pepper

- 4 bacon rashers

- 1 tbsp. oregano

- 1 tbsp. garlic powder

- 2 bread rolls stale

- 1 tbsp. parsley

- 320 grams grated cheese

- 4 sweet potatoes of medium size

- 3 spring onions

- 8 pork sausages of medium size

- 11 large eggs

- 1 bell pepper

Instructions:

1. Dice and peel the sweet potato in cubes. Mix the garlic, salt, oregano and pepper in a bowl with olive oil of extra virgin.

2. In an air fryer, put your sweet potatoes. Dice the mixed peppers, cut the sausages in quarters & dice the bacon.

3. Add the peppers, bacon and sausages over the sweet potatoes. Air fry it at 160c or 320 f for 15 mins.

4. Cube and slice the bread when your air fryer is heating & pound your eggs in a blending jug with the eggs, including some extra parsley along with pepper and salt. Dice the spring onion.

5. Check the potatoes when you hear a beep from the air fryer. A fork is needed to check on the potatoes. If you are unable to, then cook for a further 2 to 3 minutes. Mix the basket of the air fryer, include the spring onions & then cook it for an additional five minutes with the same temperature and cooking time.

6. Using the projected baking pans, place the components of your air fryer on 2 of them. Mix it while adding bread and cheese. Add your mixture of egg on them & they are primed for the actual air fry.

7. Put the baking pan inside your air fryer & cook for 25 minutes for 160 c or 320 f. If you planned to cook 2, cook 1 first and then the other one. Place a cocktail stick into the middle & then it's done if it comes out clear and clean.

11. Air fryer breakfast sausage ingredients

Cook time: 10 mins

Serving: 2 people

Difficulty: easy

Ingredients:

- 1 pound breakfast sausage

- Air fryer breakfast sausage ingredients

Instructions:

1. Insert your sausage links in the basket of an air fryer.

2. Cook your sausages or the sausage links for around 8 to 10 minutes at 360°.

12. Wake up air fryer avocado boats

Cook time: 5 mins

Servings: 2

Difficulty: easy

Ingredients:

- 1/2 teaspoon salt

- 2 plum tomatoes, seeded & diced

- 1/4 teaspoon black pepper

- 1 tablespoon finely diced jalapeno (optional)

- 4 eggs (medium or large recommended)

- 1/4 cup diced red onion

- 2 avocados, halved & pitted

- 1 tablespoon lime juice

- 2 tablespoons chopped fresh cilantro

Instructions:

1. Squeeze the avocado fruit out from the skin with a spoon, leaving the shell preserved. Dice the avocado and put it in a bowl of medium-sized. Combine it with onion, jalapeno (if there is a need), tomato, pepper and cilantro. Refrigerate and cover the mixture of avocado until ready for usage.

2. Preheat the air-fryer for 350° f

3. Place the avocado shells on a ring made up of failing to make sure they don't rock when cooking. Just roll 2 three-inch-wide strips of aluminum foil into rope shapes to create them, and turn each one into a three-inch circle. In an air fryer basket, put every avocado shell over a foil frame. Break an egg in every avocado shell & air fry for 5 - 7 minutes or when needed.

4. Take it out from the basket; fill including avocado salsa & serve.

12. Air fryer cinnamon rolls

Cook time: 15 mins

Serving: 2 people

Difficulty: easy

Ingredients:

- 1 spray must non-stick cooking spray

- 1 can cinnamon rolls we used Pillsbury

Instructions:

1. put your cinnamon rolls inside your air fryer's basket, with the help of the rounds of 2. Parchment paper or by the cooking spray that is non-stick.

2. Cook at around 340 degrees f, 171 degrees for about 12 to 15 minutes, for one time.

3. Drizzle it with icing, place it on a plate and then serve.

13. Air-fryer all-American breakfast dumplings

Cook: 10 minutes

Servings: 1 person

Difficulty: easy

Ingredients:

• Dash salt

• 1/2 cup (about four large) egg whites or liquid egg fat-free substitute

• 1 tbsp. Pre-cooked real crumbled bacon

• 1 wedge the laughing cow light creamy Swiss cheese (or 1 tbsp. reduced-fat cream cheese)

• 8 wonton wrappers or gyoza

Instructions:

1. By using a non-stick spray, spray your microwave-safe bowl or mug. Include egg whites or any substitute, salt and cheese wedge. Microwave it for around 1.5 minutes, mixing in between until cheese gets well mixed and melted and the egg is set.

2. Mix the bacon in. Let it cool completely for about 5 minutes.

3. Cover a wrapper of gyoza with the mixture of an egg (1 tablespoon). Moist the corners with water & fold it in half, having the filling. Tightly push the corners to

seal. Repeat this step to make seven more dumplings. Make sure to use a non-stick spray for spraying.

4. Insert the dumplings inside your air fryer in one single layer. (Save the leftover for another round if they all can't fit). Adjust the temperature to 375 or the closest degree. Cook it for around 5 mins or till it's crispy and golden brown.

Chapter 2: Air fryer seafood recipe

1. Air fryer 'shrimp boil'

Cook time: 15 mins

Servings: 2 people

Difficulty: easy

Ingredients:

- 2 tbsp. vegetable oil

- 1 lb. easy-peel defrosted shrimp

- 3 small red potatoes cut 1/2 inch rounds

- 1 tbsp. old bay seasoning

- 2 ears of corn cut into thirds

- 14 oz. smoked sausage, cut into three-inch pieces

Instructions:

1. Mix all the items altogether inside a huge tub & drizzle it with old bay seasoning, peppers, oil and salt. Switch to the air fryer basket attachment & place the basket over the pot.

2. Put inside your air fryer & adjust the setting of fish; make sure to flip after seven minutes.

3. Cautiously remove & then serve.

2. Air fryer fish & chips

Cook time: 10 mins

Serving: 6 people

Difficulty: easy

Ingredients:

• Tartar sauce for serving

• ½ tbsp. garlic powder

• 1 pound cod fillet cut into strips

• Black pepper

• 2 cups panko breadcrumbs

• ½ cup all-purpose flour

• ¼ tbsp. salt

• Large egg beaten

- Lemon wedges for serving

- 2 teaspoons paprika

Instructions:

1. In a tiny tub, combine the flour, adding salt, paprika and garlic powder. Put your beaten egg in one bowl & your panko breadcrumbs in another bowl.

2. Wipe your fish dry with a towel. Dredge your fish with the mixture of flour, now the egg & gradually your panko breadcrumbs, pushing down gently till your crumbs stick. Spray both ends with oil.

3. Fry at 400 degrees f. Now turn halfway for around 10 to 12 mins until it's lightly brown and crispy.

4. Open your basket & search for preferred crispiness with the help of a fork to know if it easily flakes off. You may hold fish for an extra 1 to 2 mins as required.

5. Serve instantly with tartar sauce and fries, if required.

3. Air-fryer scallops

Cook time: 20 mins

Servings: 2 people

Difficulty: easy

Ingredients:

- ¼ cup extra-virgin olive oil

- ½ tbsp. garlic finely chopped

- Cooking spray

- ½ teaspoons finely chopped garlic

- 8 large (1-oz.) Sea scallops, cleaned & patted very dry

- 1 tbsp. finely grated lemon zest

- ⅛ tbsp. salt

- 2 tbsps. Very finely chopped flat-leaf parsley

- 2 tbsp. capers, very finely chopped

- ¼ tbsp. ground pepper

Instructions:

1. Sprinkle the scallops with salt and pepper. Cover the air fryer basket by the cooking spray. Put your scallops inside the basket & cover them by the cooking spray. Put your basket inside the air fryer. Cook your scallops at a degree of 400 f till they attain the temperature of about 120 degrees f, which is an international temperature for 6 mins.

2. Mix capers, oil, garlic, lemon zest and parsley inside a tiny tub. Sprinkle over your scallops.

4. Air fryer tilapia

Cook time: 6 mins

Servings: 4 people

Difficulty: easy

Ingredients:

- 1/2 tbsp. paprika

- 1 tbsp. salt

- 2 eggs

- 4 fillets of tilapia

- 1 tbsp. garlic powder

- 1/2 teaspoon black pepper

- 1/2 cup flour

- 2 tbsp. lemon zest

- 1 tbsp. garlic powder

- 4 ounces parmesan cheese, grated

Instructions:

1. Cover your tilapia fillets:

Arrange three deep dishes. Out of these, put flour in one. Blend egg in second and make sure that the eggs are whisked in the last dish mix lemon zest, cheese, pepper, paprika and salt. Ensure that the tilapia fillets are dry, and after that dip, every fillet inside the flour & covers every side. Dip into your egg wash & pass them for coating every side of the fillet to your cheese mixture.

2. Cook your tilapia:

Put a tiny sheet of parchment paper in your bask of air fryer and put 1 - 2 fillets inside the baskets. Cook at 400°f for around 4 - 5 minutes till the crust seems golden brown, and the cheese completely melts.

5. Air fryer salmon

Cook time: 7 mins

Serving: 2 people

Difficulty: easy

Ingredients:

- 1/2 tbsp. salt

- 2 tbsp. olive oil

- 1/4 teaspoon ground black pepper

- 2 salmon fillets (about 1 1/2-inches thick)

- 1/2 teaspoon ginger powder

- 2 teaspoons smoked paprika

- 1 teaspoon onion powder

- 1/4 teaspoon red pepper flakes

- 1 tbsp. garlic powder

- 1 tablespoon brown sugar (optional)

Instructions:

1. Take the fish out of the refrigerator, check if there are any bones, & let it rest for 1 hour on the table.

2. Combine all the ingredients in a tub.

3. Apply olive oil in every fillet & then the dry rub solution.

4. Put the fillets in the Air Fryer basket.

5. set the air fryer for 7 minutes at the degree of 390 if your fillets have a thickness of 1-1/2-inches.

6. As soon as the timer stops, test fillets with a fork's help to ensure that they are ready to the perfect density. If you see that there is any need, then you cook it for a further few minutes. Your cooking time may vary with the temperature & size of the fish. It is best to set your air fryer for a minimum time, and then you may increase the time if there is a need. This will prevent the fish from being overcooked.

6. Blackened fish tacos in the air fryer

Cook time: 9 mins

Serving: 4 people

Difficulty: easy

Ingredients:

- 1 lb. Mahi mahi fillets (can use cod, catfish, tilapia or salmon)

- Cajun spices blend (or use 2-2.5 tbsp. store-bought Cajun spice blend)

- ¾ teaspoon salt

- 1 tbsp. paprika (regular, not smoked)

- 1 teaspoon oregano

- ½-¾ teaspoon cayenne (reduces or skips to preference)

- ½ teaspoon garlic powder

- ½ teaspoon onion powder

- ½ teaspoon black pepper

- 1 teaspoon brown sugar (skip for low-carb)

Additional ingredients for tacos:

- Mango salsa

- Shredded cabbage (optional)

- 8 corn tortillas

Instructions:

1. Get the fish ready

2. Mix cayenne, onion powder, brown sugar, salt, oregano, garlic powder, paprika and black pepper in a deep mixing tub.

3. Make sure to get the fish dry by using paper towels. Drizzle or brush the fish with a little amount of any cooking oil or olive oil. This allows the spices to stick to the fish.

4. Sprinkle your spice mix graciously on a single edge of your fish fillets. Rub the fish softly, so the ingredients stay on the fish.

5. Flip and brush the fish with oil on the other side & sprinkle with the leftover spices. Press the ingredients inside the fish softly.

6. Turn the air fryer on. Inside the basket put your fish fillets. Do not overlap the pan or overfill it. Close your basket.

7. Air fry the fish

8. Set your air fryer for 9 mins at 360°f. If you are using fillets which are thicker than an inch, then you must increase the cooking time to ten minutes. When the air fryer timer stops, with the help of a fish spatula or long tongs, remove your fish fillets.

9. Assembling the tacos

10. Heat the corn tortillas according to your preference. Conversely, roll them inside the towel made up of wet paper & heat them in the microwave for around 20 to 30 seconds.

11. Stack 2 small fillets or insert your fish fillet. Add a few tablespoons of your favorite mango salsa or condiment & cherish the scorched fish tacos.

12. Alternatively, one can include a few cabbages shredded inside the tacos & now add fish fillets on the top.

7. Air fryer cod

Cook time: 16 mins

Servings: 2 people

Difficulty: easy

Ingredients:

• 2 teaspoon of light oil for spraying

- 1 cup of plantain flour

- 0.25 teaspoon of salt

- 12 pieces of cod about 1 ½ pound

- 1 teaspoon of garlic powder

- 0.5 cup gluten-free flour blend

- 2 teaspoon of smoked paprika

- 4 teaspoons of Cajun seasoning or old bay

- Pepper to taste

Instructions:

1. Spray some oil on your air fryer basket & heat it up to 360° f.

2. Combine the ingredients in a tub & whisk them to blend. From your package, take the cod out and, with the help of a paper towel, pat dry.

3. Dunk every fish piece in the mixture of flour spice and flip it over & push down so that your fish can be coated.

4. Get the fish inside the basket of your air fryer. Ensure that there is room around every fish piece so that the air can flow round the fish.

5. Cook for around 8 minutes & open your air fryer so that you can flip your fish. Now cook another end for around 8 mins.

6. Now cherish the hot serving with lemon.

8. Air fryer miso-glazed Chilean sea bass

Cook time: 20 mins

Serving: 2 people

Difficulty: easy

Ingredients:

- 1/2 teaspoon ginger paste

- Fresh cracked pepper

- 1 tbsp. unsalted butter

- Olive oil for cooking

- 1 tbsp. rice wine vinegar

- 2 tbsp. miring

- 1/4 cup white miso paste

- 2 6 ounce Chilean sea bass fillets

• 4 tbsp. Maple syrup, honey works too.

Instructions:

1. Heat your air fryer to 375 degrees f. Apply olive oil onto every fish fillet and complete it with fresh pepper. Sprat olive oil on the pan of the air fryer and put the skin of the fish. Cook for about 12 to 15 minutes till you see the upper part change into golden brown color & the inner temperature now reached 135-degree f.

2. When the fish is getting cooked, you must have the butter melted inside a tiny saucepan in medium heat. When you notice that the butter melts, add maple syrup, ginger paste, miso paste, miring and rice wine vinegar, mix all of them till they are completely combined, boil them in a light flame and take the pan out instantly from the heat.

3. When your fish is completely done, brush the glaze and fish sides with the help of silicone pastry. Put it back inside your air fryer for around 1 to 2 extra minutes at 375 degrees f, till the glaze is caramelized. Complete it with green onion (sliced) & sesame seeds.

Instructions for oven

1. Heat the oven around 425 degrees f and put your baking sheet and foil sprayed with light olive oil. Bake it for about 20 to 25 minutes; this depends on how thick the fish is. The inner temperature must be around 130 degrees f when your fish is completely cooked.

2. Take out your fish, placed it in the oven & heat the broiler on a high flame. Now the fish must be brushed with miso glaze from the sides and the top & then put the fish inside the oven in the above rack. If the rack is very much near with your

broiler, then place it a bit down, you might not want the fish to touch the broiler. Cook your fish for around 1 to 2 minutes above the broiler till you see it's getting caramelize. Make sure to keep a check on it as it happens very quickly. Complete it with the help of green onions (sliced) and sesame seeds.

9. Air fryer fish tacos

Cook time: 35 mins

Serving: 6 people

Difficulty: Medium

Ingredients:

● ¼ teaspoon salt

● ¼ cup thinly sliced red onion

● 1 tbsp. water

● 2 tbsp. sour cream

● Sliced avocado, thinly sliced radishes, chopped fresh cilantro leaves and lime wedges

● 1 teaspoon lime juice

● ½ lb. skinless white fish fillets (such as halibut or mahi-mahi), cut into 1-inch strips

- 1 tbsp. mayonnaise

- 1 egg

- 1 package (12 bowls) old el Paso mini flour tortilla taco bowls, heated as directed on package

- 1 clove garlic, finely chopped

- ½ cup Progresso plain panko crispy bread crumbs

- 1 ½ cups shredded green cabbage

- 2 tbsp. old el Paso original taco seasoning mix (from 1-oz package)

Instructions:

1. Combine the sour cream, garlic, salt, mayonnaise and lime juice together in a medium pot. Add red onion and cabbage; flip to coat. Refrigerate and cover the mixture of cabbage until fit for serving.

2. Cut an 8-inch circle of parchment paper for frying. Place the basket at the bottom of the air fryer.

3. Place the taco-seasoning mix in a deep bowl. Beat the egg & water in another small bowl. Place the bread crumbs in another shallow dish. Coat the fish with your taco seasoning mix; dip inside the beaten egg, then cover with the mixture of bread crumbs, pressing to hold to it.

10. Air fryer southern fried catfish

Cook time: 13 mins

Servings: 4 people

Difficulty: easy

Ingredients:

- 1 lemon

- 1/4 teaspoon cayenne pepper

- Cornmeal seasoning mix

- 1/4 teaspoon granulated onion powder

- 1/2 cup cornmeal

- 1/2 teaspoon kosher salt

- 1/4 teaspoon chili powder

- 2 pounds catfish fillets

- 1/4 teaspoon garlic powder

- 1 cup milk

- 1/4 cup all-purpose flour

- 1/4 teaspoon freshly ground black pepper

- 2 tbsp. dried parsley flakes

- 1/2 cup yellow mustard

Instructions:

1. Add milk and put the catfish in a flat dish.

2. Slice the lemon in two & squeeze around two tbsp. of juice added into milk so that the buttermilk can be made.

3. Place the dish in the refrigerator & leave it for 15 minutes to soak the fillets.

4. Combine the cornmeal-seasoning mixture in a small bowl.

5. Take the fillets out from the buttermilk & pat them dry with the help of paper towels.

6. Spread the mustard evenly on both sides of the fillets.

7. Dip every fillet into a mixture of cornmeal & coat well to create a dense coating.

8. Place the fillets in the greased basket of the air fryer. Spray gently with olive oil.

9. Cook for around 10 minutes at 390 to 400 degrees. Turn over the fillets & spray them with oil & cook for another 3 to 5 mins.

11. Air fryer lobster tails with lemon butter

Cook time: 8 mins

Serving: 2 people

Difficulty: easy

Ingredients:

- 1 tbsp. fresh lemon juice

- 2 till 6 oz. Lobster tails, thawed

- Fresh chopped parsley for garnish (optional)

- 4 tbsp. melted salted butter

Instructions:

1. Make lemon butter combining lemon and melted butter. Mix properly & set aside.

2. Wash lobster tails & absorb the water with a paper towel. Butter your lobster tails by breaking the shell, take out the meat & place it over the shell.

3. Preheat the air fryer for around 5 minutes to 380 degrees. Place the ready lobster tails inside the basket of air fryer, drizzle with single tbsp. melted lemon butter on the meat of lobster. Cover the basket of the air fryer and cook for around 8 minutes at 380 degrees f, or when the lobster meat is not translucent. Open the air fryer halfway into the baking time, and then drizzle with extra lemon butter. Continue to bake until finished.

4. Remove the lobster tails carefully, garnish with crushed parsley if you want to, & plate. For dipping, serve with additional lemon butter.

12. Air fryer crab cakes with spicy aioli + lemon vinaigrette

Cook time: 20 mins

Servings: 2 people

Difficulty: easy

Ingredients:

For the crab cakes:

- 1. Avocado oil spray

- 16-ounce lump crab meat

- 1 egg, lightly beaten

- 2 tbsp. finely chopped red or orange pepper

- 1 tbsp. Dijon mustard

- 2 tbsp. finely chopped green onion

- 1/4 teaspoon ground pepper

- 1/4 cup panko breadcrumbs

- 2 tbsp. olive oil mayonnaise

For the aioli:

- 1/4 teaspoon cayenne pepper

- 1/4 cup olive oil mayonnaise

- 1 teaspoon white wine vinegar

- 1 teaspoon minced shallots

- 1 teaspoon Dijon mustard

For the vinaigrette:

- 2 tbsp. extra virgin olive oil

- 1 tbsp. white wine vinegar

- 4 tbsp. fresh lemon juice, about 1 ½ lemon

- 1 teaspoon honey

- 1 teaspoon lemon zest

To serve:

- Balsamic glaze, to taste

- 2 cups of baby arugula

Instructions:

1. Make your crab cake. Mix red pepper, mayonnaise, ground pepper, crab meat, onion, panko and Dijon in a huge bowl. Make sure to mix the ingredients well. Then add eggs & mix the mixture again till it's mixed well. Take around 1/4 cup of the mixture of crab into cakes which are around 1 inch thick. Spray with avocado oil gently.

2. Cook your crab cakes. Organize crab cakes in one layer in the air fryer. It depends on the air fryer how many batches will be required to cook them. Cook for 10 minutes at 375 degrees f. Take it out from your air fryer & keep it warm. Do this again if required.

3. Make aioli. Combine shallots, Dijon, vinegar, cayenne pepper and mayo. Put aside for serving until ready.

4. Make the vinaigrette. Combine honey, white vinegar, and lemon zest and lemon juice in a ting jar. Include olive oil & mix it well until mixed together.

5. Now serve. Split your arugula into 2 plates. Garnish with crab cakes. Drizzle it with vinaigrette & aioli. Include few drizzles of balsamic glaze if desired.

Chapter 3: Air Fryer Meat and Beef recipe

1. Air fryer steak

Cook time: 35 mins

Servings: 2

Difficulty: Medium

Ingredients:

- Freshly ground black pepper

- 1 tsp. freshly chopped chives

- 2 cloves garlic, minced

- 1(2 lb.) Bone-in rib eye

- 4 tbsp. Butter softened

- 1 tsp. Rosemary freshly chopped

- 2 tsp. Parsley freshly chopped

- 1 tsp. Thyme freshly chopped

- Kosher salt

Instructions:

1. In a tiny bowl, mix herbs and butter. Put a small layer of the wrap made up of plastic & roll in a log. Twist the ends altogether to make it refrigerate and tight till it gets hardened for around 20 minutes.

2. Season the steak with pepper and salt on every side.

3. Put the steak in the air-fryer basket & cook it around 400 degrees for 12 - 14 minutes, in medium temperature, depending on the thickness of the steak, tossing half-way through.

4. Cover your steak with the herb butter slice to serve.

2. Air-fryer ground beef wellington

Cook time: 20 mins

Serving: 2 people

Difficulty: easy

Ingredients:

- 1 large egg yolk

- 1 tsp. dried parsley flakes

- 2 tsp. flour for all-purpose

- 1/2 cup fresh mushrooms chopped

- 1 tbsp. butter

- 1/2 pound of ground beef

- 1 lightly beaten, large egg, it's optional

- 1/4 tsp. of pepper, divided

- 1/4 tsp. of salt

- 1 tube (having 4 ounces) crescent rolls refrigerated

- 2 tbsp. onion finely chopped

- 1/2 cup of half & half cream

Instructions:

1. Preheat the fryer to 300 degrees. Heat the butter over a moderate flame in a saucepan. Include mushrooms; stir, and cook for 5-6 minutes, until tender. Add flour & 1/8 of a tsp. of pepper when mixed. Add cream steadily. Boil it; stir and cook until thickened, for about 2 minutes. Take it out from heat & make it aside.

2. Combine 2 tbsp. of mushroom sauce, 1/8 tsp. of the remaining pepper, onion and egg yolk in a tub. Crumble over the mixture of beef and blend properly. Shape it into two loaves. Unroll and divide the crescent dough into two rectangles; push the perforations to close. Put meatloaf over every rectangle. Bring together the sides and press to seal. Brush it with one beaten egg if necessary.

3. Place the wellingtons on the greased tray inside the basket of the air fryer in a single sheet. Cook till see the thermometer placed into the meatloaf measures 160 degrees, 18 to 22 minutes and until you see golden brown color.

Meanwhile, under low pressure, warm the leftover sauce; mix in the parsley. Serve your sauce, adding wellington.

3. Air-fried burgers

Cook time: 10 mins

Serving: 4 people

Difficulty: easy

Ingredients:

- 500 g of raw ground beef (1 lb.)
- 1 tsp. of Maggi seasoning sauce
- 1/2 tsp. of ground black pepper
- 1 tsp. parsley (dried)

- Liquid smoke (some drops)

- 1/2 tsp. of salt (salt sub)

- 1 tbsp. of Worcestershire sauce

- 1/2 tsp. of onion powder

- 1/2 tsp. of garlic powder

Instructions:

1. Spray the above tray, and set it aside. You don't have to spray your basket if you are having an air fryer of basket-type. The cooking temperature for basket types will be around 180 c or 350 f.

2. Mix all the spice things together in a little tub, such as the sauce of Worcestershire and dried parsley.

2. In a huge bowl, add it inside the beef.

3. Mix properly, and make sure to overburden the meat as this contributes to hard burgers.

4. Divide the mixture of beef into four, & the patties are to be shape off. Place your indent in the middle with the thumb to keep the patties from scrunching up on the center.

5. Place tray in the air fry; gently spray the surfaces of patties.

6. Cook for around 10 minutes over medium heat (or more than that to see that your food is complete). You don't have to turn your patties.

7. Serve it hot on a pan with your array of side dishes.

4. Air fryer meatloaf

Cook time: 25 mins

Serving: 4 people

Difficulty: easy

Ingredients:

- 1/2 tsp. of Salt

- 1 tsp. of Worcestershire sauce

- 1/2 finely chopped, small onion

- 1 tbsp. of Yellow mustard

- 2 tbsp. of ketchup, divided

- 1 lb. Lean ground beef

- 1/2 tsp. Garlic powder

- 1/4 cup of dry breadcrumbs

- 1 egg, lightly beaten

- 1/4 tsp. Pepper

- 1 tsp. Italian seasoning

Instructions:

1. Put the onion, 1 tbsp. Ketchup, garlic powder, pepper, ground beef, egg, salt, breadcrumbs, Italian seasoning and Worcestershire sauce in a huge bowl.

2. Use hands to blend your spices with the meat equally, be careful you don't over-mix as it would make it difficult to over mix.

3. Shape meat having two inches height of 4 by 6, loaf. Switch your air fryer to a degree of 370 f & Put that loaf inside your air fryer.

4. Cook for fifteen min at a degree of 370 f.

5. In the meantime, mix the leftover 1 tbsp. of ketchup & the mustard in a tiny bowl.

6. Take the meatloaf out of the oven & spread the mixture of mustard over it.

7. Return the meatloaf to your air fryer & begin to bake at a degree of 370 degrees f till the thermometer placed inside the loaf measures 160 degrees f, around 8 to 10 further minutes.

8. Remove the basket from your air fryer when the meatloaf has touched 160 degrees f & then make the loaf stay inside the air fryer basket for around 5 to 10 minutes, after that slice your meatloaf.

5. Air fryer hamburgers

Cook time: 16 mins

Serving: 4 people

Difficulty: easy

Ingredients:

- 1 tsp. of onion powder

- 1 pound of ground beef (we are using 85/15)

- 4 pieces burger buns

- 1 tsp. salt

- 1/4 tsp. of black pepper

- 1 tsp. of garlic powder

- 1 tsp. of Worcestershire sauce

Instructions:

1. Method for standard ground beef:

2. Your air fryer must be preheated to 360 °.

3. In a bowl, put the unprocessed ground beef & add the seasonings.

4. To incorporate everything, make the of use your hands (or you can use a fork) & then shape the mixture in a ball shape (still inside the bowl).

5. Score the mixture of ground beef into 4 equal portions by having a + mark to split it.

Scoop out and turn each segment into a patty.

6. Place it in the air fryer, ensuring each patty has plenty of room to cook (make sure not to touch). If required, one can perform this in groups. We've got a bigger (5.8 quart) air fryer, and we did all of ours in a single batch.

7. Cook, turning half-way back, for 16 minutes. (Note: for bigger patties, you may have a need to cook longer.)

Process for Patties (pre-made):

1. In a tiny bowl, mix onion powder, pepper, garlic powder and salt, then stir till well mixed.

2. In a tiny bowl, pour in a few quantities of Worcestershire sauce. You may require A little more than one teaspoon (such as 1.5 tsp.), as some of it will adhere in your pastry brush.

3. Put patties on a tray & spoon or brush on a thin layer of your Worcestershire sauce.

4. Sprinkle with seasoning on every patty, saving 1/2 for another side.

5. With your hand, rub the seasoning to allow it to stick better.

6. Your air fryer should be preheated to 360 ° f.

7. Take out the basket when it's preheated & gently place your patties, seasoned one down, inside the basket.

8. Side 2 of the season, which is facing up the exact way as per above.

9. In an air fryer, put the basket back and cook for around 16 minutes, tossing midway through.

6. Air Fryer Meatloaf

Cook time: 25 mins

Serving: 4 people

Difficulty: Easy

Ingredients:

• Ground black pepper for taste

• 1 tbsp. of olive oil, or as required

• 1 egg, lightly beaten

• 1 tsp. of salt

• 1 pound of lean ground beef

• 1 tbsp. fresh thyme chopped

• 3 tbsp. of dry bread crumbs

• 1 finely chopped, small onion

• 2 thickly sliced mushrooms

Instructions:

1. Preheat your air fryer to a degree of 392 f (200°C).

2. Mix together egg, onion, salt, ground beef, pepper, bread crumbs and thyme in a tub. 3. Thoroughly knead & mix.

4. Transfer the mixture of beef in your baking pan & smooth out the surface. The mushrooms are to be pressed from the top & coated with the olive oil. Put the pan inside the basket of the air fryer & slide it inside your air fryer.

5. Set the timer of the air fryer for around 25 minutes & roast the meatloaf till it is nicely browned.

6. Make sure that the meatloaf stays for a minimum of 10 minutes, and after that, you can slice and serve.

7. Air Fryer Beef Kabobs

Cook time: 8 mins

Serving: 4 people

Difficulty: Easy

Ingredients:

• 1 big onion in red color or onion which you want

• 1.5 pounds of sirloin steak sliced into one-inch chunks

• 1 large bell pepper of your choice

For the marinade:

- 1 tbsp. of lemon juice

- Pinch of Salt & pepper

- 4 tbsp. of olive oil

- 1/2 tsp. of cumin

- 1/2 tsp. of chili powder

- 2 cloves garlic minced

Ingredients:

1. In a huge bowl, mix the beef & ingredients to marinade till fully mixed. Cover & marinate for around 30 minutes or up to 24 hours inside the fridge.

2. Preheat your air fryer to a degree of 400 f until prepared to cook. Thread the onion, pepper and beef onto skewers.

3. Put skewers inside the air fryer, which is already heated and the air fryer for about 8 to 10 minutes, rotating half-way until the outside is crispy and the inside is tender.

8. Air-Fried Beef and Vegetable Skewers

Cook time: 8 mins

Serving: 2

Difficulty: easy

Ingredients:

- 2 tbs. of olive oil

- 2 tsp. of fresh cilantro chopped

- Kosher salt & freshly black pepper ground

- 1 tiny yellow summer squash, sliced into one inch (of 2.5-cm) pieces

- 1/4 tsp. of ground coriander

- Lemon wedges to serve (optional)

- 1/8 tsp. of red pepper flakes

- 1 garlic clove, minced

- 1/2 tsp. of ground cumin

- 1/2 yellow bell pepper, sliced into one inch (that's 2.5-cm) pieces

- 1/2 red bell pepper, sliced into one inch (that's 2.5-cm) pieces

- 1/2 lb. (that's 250 g) boneless sirloin, sliced into one inch (of 2.5-cm) cubes

- 1 tiny zucchini, sliced into one inch (that's 2.5-cm) pieces

- 1/2 red onion, sliced into one inch (that's 2.5-cm) pieces

Ingredients:

1. Preheat your air fryer at 390 degrees f (199-degree c).

2. In a tiny bowl, mix together one tablespoon of cumin, red pepper flakes and coriander. Sprinkle the mixture of spices generously over the meat.

3. In a tub, mix together zucchini, oil, cilantro, bell peppers, summer squash, cilantro, onion and garlic. Season with black pepper and salt to taste.

4. Tightly thread the vegetables and meat onto the four skewers adding two layers rack of air fryer, rotating the bits and equally splitting them. Put the skewers over the rack & carefully set your rack inside the cooking basket. Put the basket inside the air fryer. Cook, without covering it for around 7 - 8 minutes, till the vegetables are crispy and tender & your meat is having a medium-rare.

5. Move your skewers to a tray, and if you want, you can serve them with delicious lemon wedges.

9. Air fryer taco calzones

Cook time: 10 mins

Serving: 2 people

Difficulty: easy

Ingredients:

- 1 cup of taco meat

- 1 tube of Pillsbury pizza dough thinly crust

- 1 cup of shredded cheddar

Instructions:

1. Spread out the layer of your pizza dough over a clean table. Slice the dough into four squares with the help of a pizza cutter.

2. By the use of a pizza cutter, cut every square into a big circle. Place the dough pieces aside to create chunks of sugary cinnamon.

3. Cover 1/2 of every dough circle with around 1/4 cup of taco meat & 1/4 cup of shredded cheese.

4. To seal it firmly, fold the remaining over the cheese and meat and push the sides of your dough along with the help of a fork so that it can be tightly sealed. Repeat for all 4 calzones.

5. Each calzone much is gently picked up & spray with olive oil or pan spray. Organize them inside the basket of Air Fryer.

Cook your calzones at a degree of 325 for almost 8 to 10 minutes. Monitor them carefully when it reaches to 8 min mark. This is done so that there is no chance of overcooking.

6. Using salsa & sour cream to serve.

7. For the making of cinnamon sugary chunks, split the dough pieces into pieces having equal sides of around 2 inches long. Put them inside the basket of the air fryer & cook it at a degree of 325 for around 5 minutes. Instantly mix with the one ratio four sugary cinnamon mixtures.

10. Air Fryer Pot Roast

Cook time: 30 mins

Serving: 2 people

Difficulty: Medium

Ingredients:

- 1 tsp. of salt

- 3 tbsp. of brown sugar

- 1/2 cup of orange juice

- 1 tsp. of Worcestershire sauce

- 1/2 tsp. of pepper

- 3–4 pound thawed roast beef chuck roast

- 3 tbsp. of soy sauce

Instructions:

1. Combine brown sugar, Worcestershire sauce, soy sauce and orange juice.

2. Mix till the sugar is completely dissolved.

3. Spillover the roast & marinade for around 8 to 24 hours.

4. Put the roast in the basket of an air fryer.

5. Sprinkle the top with pepper and salt.

6. Air fry it at a degree of 400 f for around 30 minutes, turning it half-way through.

7. Allow it to pause for a period of 3 minutes.

8. Slice and serve into thick cuts.

Chapter 4: midnight snacks

1. Air fryer onion rings

Cook time: 7 mins

Serving: 2 people

Difficulty: easy

Ingredients:

- 2 beaten, large eggs

- Marinara sauce for serving

- 1 ½ tsp. of kosher salt

- ½ tsp. of garlic powder

- 1 medium yellow onion, cut into half in about (1 1/4 cm)

- 1 cup of flour for all-purpose (125 g)

- 1 ½ cups of panko breadcrumbs (172 g)

- 1 tsp. of paprika

- ⅛ tsp. of cayenne

- ½ tsp. of onion powder

- ½ tsp. black pepper freshly ground

Instructions:

1. Preheat your air fryer to 190°c (375°f).

2. Use a medium-size bowl to mix together onion powder, salt, paprika, cayenne, pepper, flour and garlic powder.

3. In 2 separate small cups, add your panko & eggs.

4. Cover onion rings with flour, then with the eggs, and afterward with the panko.

Working in lots, put your onion rings in one layer inside your air fryer & "fry" for 5 to 7 minutes or till you see golden brown color.

5. Using warm marinara sauce to serve.

2. Air fryer sweet potato chips

Cook time: 15 mins

Serving: 2

Difficulty: easy

Ingredients:

- 1 ½ tsp. of kosher salt

- 1 tsp. of dried thyme

- 1 large yam or sweet potato

- ½ tsp. of pepper

- 1 tbsp. of olive oil

Instructions:

1. Preheat your air fryer to a degree of 350 f (180 c).

2. Slice your sweet potato have a length of 3- to 6-mm (1/8-1/4-inch). In a medium tub, mix your olive oil with slices of sweet potato until well-seasoned. Add some pepper, thyme and salt to cover.

3. Working in groups, add your chips in one sheet & fry for around 14 minutes till you see a golden brown color and slightly crisp.

Fun.

3. Air fryer tortilla chips

Cook time: 5 mins

Serving: 2 people

Difficulty: easy

Ingredients:

- 1 tbsp. of olive oil

- Guacamole for serving

- 2 tsp. of kosher salt

- 12 corn of tortillas

- 1 tbsp. of McCormick delicious jazzy spice blend

Instructions:

1. Preheat your air fryer at a degree of 350 f (180 c).

2. Gently rub your tortillas with olive oil on every side.

3. Sprinkle your tortillas with delicious jazzy spice and salt mix on every side.

Slice every tortilla into six wedges.

4. Functioning in groups, add your tortilla wedges inside your air fryer in one layer & fry it for around 5 minutes or until you see golden brown color and crispy texture.

Serve adding guacamole

4. Air fryer zesty chicken wings

Cook time: 20 mins

Serving: 2 people

Difficulty: easy

Ingredients:

- 1 ½ tsp. of kosher salt

- 1 ½ lb. of patted dry chicken wings (of 680 g)

- 1 tbsp. of the delicious, zesty spice blend

Instructions:

1. Preheat your air fryer at 190°c (375°f).

2. In a tub, get your chicken wings mixed in salt & delicious zesty spice, which must be blend till well-seasoned.

3. Working in lots, add your chicken wings inside the air fryer in one layer & fry it for almost 20 minutes, turning it halfway through.

4. Serve it warm

5. Air fryer sweet potato fries

Cook time: 15 mins

Serving: 2 people

Difficulty: easy

Ingredients:

- 1/4 tsp. of sea salt

- 1 tbsp. of olive oil

- 2 (having 6-oz.) sweet potatoes, cut & peeled into sticks of 1/4-inch

- Cooking spray

- 1/4 tsp. of garlic powder

- 1 tsp. fresh thyme chopped

Instructions:

1. Mix together thyme, garlic powder, olive oil and salt in a bowl. Put sweet potato inside the mixture and mix well to cover.

2. Coat the basket of the air fryer gently with the help of cooking spray. Place your sweet potatoes in one layer inside the basket & cook in groups at a degree of 400 f until soft inside & finely browned from outside for around 14 minutes, rotating the fries halfway through the cooking process.

6. Air fryer churros with chocolate sauce

Cook time: 30 mins

Serving: 12

Difficulty: easy

Ingredients:

- 1/4 cup, adding 2 tbsp. Unsalted butter that's divided into half-cup (around 2 1/8 oz.)

- 3 tbsp. of heavy cream

- Half cup water

- 4 ounces of bitter and sweet finely chopped baking chocolate

- Flour for All-purpose

- 2 tsp. of ground cinnamon

- 2 large eggs

- 1/4 tsp. of kosher salt

- 2 tbsp. of vanilla kefir

- 1/3 cup of granulated sugar

Instruction:

1. Bring salt, water & 1/4 cup butter and boil it in a tiny saucepan with a medium-high flame. Decrease the heat to around medium-low flame; add flour & mix actively with a spoon made up of wood for around 30 seconds.

2. Stir and cook continuously till the dough is smooth. Do this till you see your dough continues to fall away from the sides of the pan & a film appears on the bottom of the pan after 2 to 3 minutes. Move the dough in a medium-sized bowl. Stir continuously for around 1 minute until slightly cooled. Add one egg from time to time while stirring continuously till you see it gets smoother after every addition. Move the mixture in the piping bag, which is fitted with having star tip of medium size. Chill it for around 30 minutes.

3. Pipe 6 (3" long) bits in one-layer inside a basket of the air fryer. Cook at a degree of 380 f for around 10 minutes. Repeat this step for the leftover dough.

4. Stir the sugar & cinnamon together inside a medium-size bowl. Use 2 tablespoons of melted butter to brush the cooked churros. Cover them with the sugar mixture.

THE ULTIMATE AIR FRYER BIBLE [4 IN 1] BY MICHELLE POLPETTA

5. Put the cream and chocolate in a tiny, microwaveable tub. Microwave with a high temperature for roughly 30 seconds until molten and flat, stirring every 15 seconds. Mix in kefir.

6. Serve the churros, including chocolate sauce.

7. Whole-wheat pizzas in an air fryer

Cook time: 10 mins

Serving: 2 people

Difficulty: easy

Ingredients:

- 1 small thinly sliced garlic clove

- 1/4 ounce of Parmigiano-Reggiano shaved cheese (1 tbsp.)

- 1 cup of small spinach leaves (around 1 oz.)

- 1/4 cup marinara sauce (lower-sodium)

- 1-ounce part-skim pre-shredded mozzarella cheese (1/4 cup)

- 1 tiny plum tomato, sliced into 8 pieces

- 2 pita rounds of whole-wheat

Instructions:

1. Disperse marinara sauce equally on one side of every pita bread. Cover it each with half of the tomato slices, cheese, spinach leaves and garlic.

2. Put 1 pita in the basket of air-fryer & cook it at a degree of 350 f until the cheese is melted and the pita is crispy. Repeat with the leftover pita.

8. Air-fried corn dog bites

Cook time: 15 mins

Serving: 4 people

Difficulty: easy

Ingredients:

- 2 lightly beaten large eggs

- 2 uncured hot dogs of all-beef

- Cooking spray

- 12 bamboo skewers or craft sticks

- 8 tsp. of yellow mustard

- 1 1/2 cups cornflakes cereal finely crushed

- 1/2 cup (2 1/8 oz.) Flour for All-purpose

Instructions:

1. Split lengthwise every hot dog. Cut every half in three same pieces. Add a bamboo skewer or the craft stick inside the end of every hot dog piece.

2. Put flour in a bowl. Put slightly beaten eggs in another shallow bowl. Put crushed cornflakes inside another shallow bowl. Mix the hot dogs with flour; make sure to shake the surplus. Soak in the egg, helping you in dripping off every excess. Dredge inside the cornflakes crumbs, pushing to stick.

3. Gently coat the basket of the air fryer with your cooking spray. Put around six bites of corn dog inside the basket; spray the surface lightly with the help of cooking spray. Now cook at a degree of 375 f till the coating shows a golden

brown color and is crunchy for about 10 minutes, flipping the bites of corn dog halfway in cooking. Do this step with other bites of the corn dog.

4. Put three bites of corn dog with 2 tsp. of mustard on each plate to, and then serve immediately.

9. Crispy veggie quesadillas in an air fryer

Cook time: 20 mins

Serving: 4 people

Difficulty: easy

Instructions:

• Cooking spray

• 1/2 cup refrigerated and drained pico de gallo

• 4 ounces far educing cheddar sharp cheese, shredded (1 cup)

• 1 tbsp. of fresh juice (with 1 lime)

• 4(6-in.) whole-grain Sprouted flour tortillas

• 1/4 tsp. ground cumin

• 2 tbsp. fresh cilantro chopped

• 1 cup red bell pepper sliced

• 1 cup of drained & rinsed black beans canned, no-salt-added

• 1 tsp. of lime zest plus

• 1 cup of sliced zucchini

• 2 ounces of plain 2 percent fat reduced Greek yogurt

Instructions:

1. Put tortillas on the surface of your work. Sprinkle two tbsp. Shredded cheese on the half of every tortilla. Each tortilla must be top with cheese, having a cup of 1/4 each black beans, slices of red pepper equally and zucchini slices. Sprinkle equally with the leftover 1/2 cup of cheese. Fold the tortillas making a shape of a half-moon. Coat quesadillas lightly with the help of cooking spray & protect them with toothpicks.

2. Gently spray the cooking spray on the basket of the air fryer. Cautiously put two quesadillas inside the basket & cook it at a degree of 400 f till the tortillas are of golden brown color & slightly crispy, vegetables get softened, and the cheese if finally melted for around 10 minutes, rotating the quesadillas halfway while cooking. Do this step again with the leftover quesadillas.

3. As the quesadillas are cooking, mix lime zest, cumin, yogurt and lime juice altogether in a small tub. For serving, cut the quesadilla in slices & sprinkle it with cilantro. Serve it with a tablespoon of cumin cream and around 2 tablespoons of pico de gallo.

10. Air-fried curry chickpeas

Cook time: 10 mins

Serving: 4 people

Difficulty: easy

Ingredients:

- 2 tbsp. of curry powder

- Fresh cilantro thinly sliced

- 1(15-oz.) Can chickpeas (like garbanzo beans), rinsed & drained (1 1/2 cups)

- 1/4 tsp. of kosher salt

- 1/2 tbsp. of ground turmeric

- 1/2 tsp. of Aleppo pepper

- 1/4 tsp. of ground coriander

- 2 tbsp. of olive oil

- 1/4 tsp. and 1/8 tsp. of Ground cinnamon

- 2 tbsp. of vinegar (red wine)

- 1/4 tsp. of ground cumin

Instructions:

1. Smash chickpeas softly inside a tub with your hands (don't crush); remove chickpea skins.

2. Apply oil and vinegar to chickpeas, & toss for coating. Add turmeric, cinnamon, cumin, curry powder and coriander; whisk gently so that they can be mixed together.

3. Put chickpeas in one layer inside the bask of air fryer & cook at a degree of 400 f till it's crispy for around 15 mins; shake the chickpeas timely while cooking.

4. Place the chickpeas in a tub. Sprinkle it with cilantro, Aleppo pepper and salt; blend to coat.

11. Air fry shrimp spring rolls with sweet chili sauce.

Cook time: 20 mins

Serving: 4

Difficulty: easy

Ingredients:

- 1 cup of matchstick carrots

- 8 (8" square) wrappers of spring roll

- 2 1/2 tbsp. of divided sesame oil

- 4 ounces of peeled, deveined and chopped raw shrimp

- 1/2 cup of chili sauce (sweet)

- 1 cup of (red) bell pepper julienne-cut

- 2 tsp. of fish sauce

- 3/4 cup snow peas julienne-cut

- 2 cups of cabbage, pre-shredded

- 1/4 tsp. of red pepper, crushed

- 1 tbsp. of lime juice (fresh)

- 1/4 cup of fresh cilantro (chopped)

Instructions:

1. In a large pan, heat around 1 1/2 tsp. of oil until softly smoked. Add carrots, bell pepper and cabbage; Cook, stirring constantly, for 1 to 1 1/2 minutes, until finely wilted. Place it on a baking tray; cool for 5 minutes.

2. In a wide tub, place the mixture of cabbage, snow peas, cilantro, fish sauce, red pepper, shrimp and lime juice; toss to blend.

3. Put the wrappers of spring roll on the surface with a corner that is facing you. Add a filling of 1/4 cup in the middle of every wrapper of spring roll, extending from left-hand side to right in a three-inch wide strip.

4. Fold each wrapper's bottom corner over the filling, stuffing the corner tip under the filling. Fold the corners left & right over the filling. Brush the remaining corner softly with water; roll closely against the remaining corner; press gently to cover. Use 2 teaspoons of the remaining oil to rub the spring rolls.

5. Inside the basket of air fryer, put four spring rolls & cook at a degree of 390 f till it's golden, for 6 - 7 minutes, rotating the spring rolls every 5 minutes. Repeat with the leftover spring rolls. Use chili sauce to serve.

Chapter 5: Dessert recipes

1. Air fryer mores

Cook time: 2 mins

Serving: 2 people

Difficulty: easy

Ingredients:

- 1 big marshmallow

- 2 graham crackers split in half

- 2 square, fine quality chocolate

Instructions:

1. Preheat the air fryer at a degree of 330 f.

2. When preheating, break 2 graham crackers into two to form four squares. Cut 1 big marshmallow into half evenly so that one side can be sticky.

3. Add every half of your marshmallow in a square of one graham cracker & push downwards to stick the marshmallow with graham cracker. You must now have two marshmallows coated with graham crackers & two regular graham crackers.

4. In one layer, put two graham crackers and marshmallows inside your air fryer & cook for about 2 minutes till you can see the marshmallow becoming toasted slightly.

5. Remove immediately and completely and add 1 chocolate square to the toasted marshmallow. Add the rest of the squares of the graham cracker and press down. Enjoy instantly.

2. Easy air fryer brownies

Cook time: 15 mins

Serving: 4 people

Difficulty: easy

Ingredients:

- 2 large eggs

- ½ cup flour for all-purpose

- ¼ cup melted unsalted butter

- 6 tbsp. of cocoa powder, unsweetened

- ¼ tsp. of baking powder

- ¾ cup of sugar

- ½ tsp. of vanilla extract

- 1 tbsp. of vegetable oil

- ¼ tsp. of salt

Instructions:

1. Get the 7-inch baking tray ready by gently greasing it with butter on all the sides and even the bottom. Put it aside

2. Preheat the air fryer by adjusting its temperature to a degree of 330 f & leaving it for around 5 minutes as you cook the brownie batter.

3. Add baking powder, cocoa powder, vanilla extract, flour for all-purpose, butter, vegetable oil, salt, eggs and sugar in a big tub & mix it unless well combined.

4. Add up all these for the preparation of the baking pan & clean the top.

5. Put it inside the air fryer & bake it for about 15 minutes or as long as a toothpick can be entered and comes out easily from the center.

6. Take it out and make it cool in the tray until you remove and cut.

3. Easy air fryer churros

Cook time: 5 mins

Serving: 4 people

Difficulty: easy

Ingredients:

- 1 tbsp. of sugar

- Sifted powdered sugar & cinnamon or cinnamon sugar

- 1 cup (about 250ml) water

- 4 eggs

- ½ cup (113g) butter

- ¼ tsp. salt

- 1 cup (120g) all-purpose flour

Instructions:

1. Mix the ingredients bringing them to boil while stirring continuously.

2. Add flour & start mixing properly. Take it out from the heat & mix it till it gets smooth & the dough can be taken out from the pan easily.

3. Add one egg at one time and stir it until it gets smooth. Set it to cool.

4. Preheat your air fryer degree of 400 for 200 c.

5. Cover your bag of cake decorations with dough & add a star tip of 1/2 inch.

6. Make sticks which are having a length of 3 to 4 inches by moving your dough out from the bag in paper (parchment). You can now switch it inside your air fryer if you are ready to do so. If it is hard to handle the dough, put it inside the refrigerator for around 30 minutes.

7. Use cooking spray or coconut oil to spray the tray or the basket of your air fryer.

8. Add around 8 to 10 churros in a tray or inside the basket of the air fryer. Spray with oil.

9. Cook for 5 minutes at a degree of 400 for 200 c.

10. Until finished and when still hot, rill in regular sugar, cinnamon or sugar mixture.

11. Roll in the cinnamon-sugar blend, cinnamon or normal sugar until finished and when still high.

4. Air fryer sweet apples

Cook time: 8 mins

Serving: 4 people

Difficulty: easy

Ingredients:

- ¼ cup of white sugar

- ⅓ Cup of water

- ¼ cup of brown sugar

- ½ tsp. of ground cinnamon

- 6 apples diced and cored

- ¼ tsp. of pumpkin pie spice

- ¼ tsp. of ground cloves

Instructions:

1. Put all the ingredients in a bowl that is oven safe & combine it with water and seasonings. Put the bowl inside the basket, oven tray or even in the toaster of an air fryer.

2. Air fry the mixture of apples at a degree of 350 f for around 6 minutes. Mix the apples & cook them for an extra 2 minutes. Serve it hot and enjoy.

5. Air fryer pear crisp for two

Cook time: 20 mins

Serving: 2

Difficulty: easy

Ingredients:

- ¾ tsp. of divided ground cinnamon

- 1 tbsp. of softened salted butter

- 1 tsp. of lemon juice

- 2 pears. Peeled, diced and cored

- 1 tbsp. of flour for all-purpose

- 2 tbsp. of quick-cooking oats

- 1 tbsp. of brown sugar

Instructions:

1. Your air fryer should be preheated at a degree of 360 f (180 c).

2. Mix lemon juice, 1/4 tsp. Cinnamon and pears in a bowl. Turn for coating and then split the mixture into 2 ramekins.

3. Combine brown sugar, oats, leftover cinnamon and flour in the tub. Using your fork to blend in the melted butter until the mixture is mushy. Sprinkle the pears.

4. Put your ramekins inside the basket of an air fryer & cook till the pears become bubbling and soft for around 18 - 20 minutes.

6. Keto chocolate cake – air fryer recipe

Cook time: 10 mins

Serving: 6 people

Difficulty: easy

Ingredients:

- 1 tsp. of vanilla extract

- 1/2 cup of powdered Swerve

- 1/3 cup of cocoa powder unsweetened

- 1/4 tsp. of salt

- 1 & 1/2 cups of almond flour

- 2 large eggs

- 1/3 cups of almond milk, unsweetened

- 1 tsp. of baking powder

Instructions:

1. In a big mixing tub, mix every ingredient until they all are well mixed.

2. Butter or spray your desired baking dish. We used bunt tins in mini size, but you can even get a 6-inch cake pan in the baskets of the air fryer.

3. Scoop batter equally inside your baking dish or dishes.

4. Set the temperature of the air fryer to a degree of 350 f & set a 10-minute timer. Your cake will be ready when the toothpick you entered comes out clear and clean.

Conclusion:

The air fryer seems to be a wonderful appliance that will assist you with maintaining your diet. You will also enjoy the flavor despite eating high amounts of oil if you prefer deep-fried food.

Using a limited quantity of oil, you will enjoy crunchy & crispy food without the additional adverse risk, which tastes exactly like fried food. Besides, the system is safe & easy to use. All you must do is choose the ingredients needed, and there will be nutritious food available for your family.

An air fryer could be something which must be considered if a person is attempting to eat a diet having a lower-fat diet, access to using the system to prepare a range of foods, & want trouble cooking experience.

The Mediterranean Diet Cookbook with Pictures

Tens of Tasty Recipes to Shed Weight and Feel Great in 2021

Michelle Polpetta

Contents

Introduction

Many people may think about "a diet" as a particular weight reduction plan; however diet just alludes to the sorts and measures of food an individual eats. An empowering diet should incorporate equilibrium of a few nutrition classes, as no single gathering can give all the body requires to great wellbeing. Settling on healthy food decisions decreases an individual's danger of numerous persistent medical issues, including cardiovascular illness, two types of diabetes, and disease. There is an abundance of data accessible, so planning a reasonable, restorative diet can feel overpowering. All things considered, a couple of straightforward changes can make a diet more nutritious and decrease the danger of numerous clinical issues. Eating great is central to acceptable wellbeing and prosperity. Healthy eating causes us to keep a healthy weight and lessens our danger of type 2 diabetes, hypertension, elevated cholesterol and the danger of creating cardiovascular sickness and a few tumors.

Healthy diet

Healthy eating has numerous different advantages. At the point when we eat well we rest better, have more energy and better fixation and this all amounts to better, more joyful lives! Healthy eating ought to be a pleasant social encounter. At the point when kids and youngsters eat and drink well they get all the fundamental supplements they require for legitimate development and improvement, and build up a decent connection with food and other social abilities.

Healthy diet isn't tied in with removing nourishments it's tied in with eating a wide assortment of food sources in the perfect adds up to give your body what it needs. There are no single nourishments you should eat or menus you need to follow to eat strongly. You simply need to ensure you get the correct equilibrium of various food sources. Healthy eating for youngsters and youngsters ought to consistently incorporate a scope of fascinating and scrumptious food that can make up a healthy, differed and adjusted diet, as opposed to denying them certain nourishments and beverages. Albeit everything food sources can be remembered for a healthy diet, this won't be valid for individuals on uncommon/clinical diets.

Healthy diets assists individuals with keeping up and improve their overall wellbeing. It is imperative to allow the correct supplements every day to acquire a healthy diet. Supplements can be gotten in numerous food sources and a huge number of diet plans. It is significant that individuals watch their admission of diet plans. It is significant that individuals watch their admission of food to keep a healthy diet. Having an unhealthy diet can be a significant danger factor for various persistent infections including hypertension, weight, and diabetes. It's vital to realize how to bring down hypertension since it's a condition that builds the danger for coronary episode, stroke, kidney disappointment, and other medical issues. The decisions we make in our way of life can go far towards forestalling hypertension. Individuals, who don't as of now have hypertension, should get comfortable with healthy propensities to diminish their danger of truly getting it. Individuals, who as of now have hypertension, ought to quickly begin healthy propensities to bring down their pulse and decline their danger of creating significant complexities. Overseeing pressure is significant in light of the fact that pressure can cause significant damage anybody and it can assume a critical part in hypertension.

Importance of healthy diet

The significance of devouring the appropriate diet can't be focused on enough, particularly as we age. The nourishments that we decide to eat every day can have various impacts on the brain and body and can have a tremendous effect on our mind-set and ways of life. Albeit as a rule we may end up battling to oppose that thicker style skillet select pizza, picking a better option can truly pay off! Rehearsing a healthy diet and reliably devouring the correct supplements can have five significant effects, among numerous others!

Keep up Normal Body Function

As we age, you may see that you can't hear very too or experience difficulty recollecting straightforward notes that in earlier years would have been no issue! In all honesty, our diet can significantly affect numerous substantial capacities. These including your five detect, pH level, pulse, glucose level, the capacity to modify tissues and your equilibrium. Rehearsing a healthy diet can assist you with keeping up these body capacities as you keep on maturing.

Keep up Healthy Weight

This one ought to be an easy decision. In the event that you eat seared food consistently you won't seem as though the conditioned bodies you find in wellness magazines. Not exclusively does eating healthy hold your weight down, it additionally lessens the danger of coronary illness, diabetes and irregular circulatory strain.

Forestall Diseases

At the point when you eat a balanced diet including an assortment of foods grown from the ground, lean proteins and entire grains that are low in trans and soaked fat, you are diminishing the danger of becoming ill and creating persistent infections like cardiovascular and diabetes.

Mind-set and Energy

An even diet influences your body and its capacities, however your psyche also. Nutrients assume a part in the activity of synapses and insufficiencies that can prompt gloom and state of mind problems. Great nourishment can likewise support your energy level, which than thusly can help you complete your day by day schedule easily, eventually bringing about a superior mind-set – so eat great food!

Give Stress Relief

Like the effect nutrients have on your state of mind, legitimate sustenance can likewise give pressure alleviation by lessening the results of medicine, boosting the insusceptible framework, and can assist you with keeping up quieting and adapting capacities.

WHAT and WHEN to Eat

With presence of mind the vast majority can sort out what to eat and what not to eat. Leafy foods give the fundamental nutrients expected to a healthy diet and are in every case bravo. Lean proteins, for example, egg whites, yogurt, salmon, fish and other ocean nourishments and chicken bosom are generally incredible models. Leafy foods, sugars, lean protein, and nutrients and minerals are for the most part key fixings to a healthy way of life. Shockingly, WHAT you eat is a large portion of the fight. The WHEN is nearly pretty much as significant as the substance of the food sources you pick. It is significant not to over-eat, implying that you should customer more modest bits of food for the duration of the day. Breakfast, lunch and supper ought not to be skipped, yet make certain to nibble on a yogurt, banana or fiber bar in the middle of dinners. Eating more modest parts of food all through the whole day will accelerate your digestion and keep you strong and smart.

Balanced Diet

An individual needs proper measures of proteins, minerals, and supplements in a balanced diet. It is very essential for the smooth working of our body. In the event that we devour a balanced diet consistently, we will consistently stay healthy. It reduces any odds of becoming sick. Additionally, a balanced diet likewise supports our insusceptibility framework.

Significance of a Balanced Diet

The vast majority accept that a balanced diet is certainly the way in to a healthy way of life. It is appropriately accepted as even researchers say as much. At the point when we generally devour a balanced diet, we will keep up our physical just as emotional well-being. A balanced diet should contain the legitimate food sources that are burned-through in well-suited amounts. An ideal balanced diet is made out of carbs, proteins, fats, minerals, high fiber substance, nutrients, and then some.

In addition, these days the pattern of shoddy nourishment is staying put. Individuals are not taking a balanced diet rather eating a wide range of unsafe nourishments. It is a higher priority than at any other time to enlighten individuals regarding the significance of a balanced diet. You can't simply practice and anticipate that your body should remain fit. A balanced diet is significant for that.

Above all, it is known as a 'balanced' diet since it requires all the food sources to be eaten in a balanced way. For example, in the event that you admission a lot of sugars and a little measure of protein, at that point that won't be known as a balanced diet, regardless of whether you are eating the correct nourishments. The equilibrium should be kept up for that.

Besides, these days the pattern of lousy nourishment is setting down deep roots. Individuals are not taking a balanced diet rather eating a wide range of hurtful food sources. It is a higher priority than at any other time to inform individuals regarding the significance of a balanced diet. You can't simply practice and anticipate that your body should remain fit. A balanced diet is vital for that.

In particular, it is known as a 'balanced' diet since it requires all the food sources to be eaten in a balanced way. For example, in the event that you intake a lot of sugars and a little measure of protein, at that point that won't be known as a balanced diet, regardless of whether you are eating the correct food sources. The equilibrium should be kept up for that.

The Mediterranean Diet

In the event that you've at any point conversed with someone after they've ventured out to a country like Italy or Greece, they presumably referenced how delightful the food was. Food is one of the more normal affiliations with nations that encompass the Mediterranean Sea; and naturally so. The food this locale produces is striking to such an extent that there is a diet based off it, companied with perpetual examination expounding the medical advantages it obliges. Fittingly named The Mediterranean Diet, this gathering of food sources including fish, natural products, vegetables, beans, high fiber breads, entire grains, nuts, olive oil and red wine are focused to help forestall various infections just as advance wellbeing in various areas of the body. This book will address every segment, advantage, and precautionary measure of the Mediterranean diet, top to bottom, all with a primary spotlight on the dietary variables.

Basics

The Mediterranean diet is anything but a solitary diet but instead an eating design that takes motivation from the diet of southern European nations. There is an accentuation on plant food sources, olive oil, fish, poultry, beans, and grains.

The diet draws together the basic food types and empowering propensities from the conventions of a few distinct locales, including Greece, Spain, southern France, Portugal, and Italy.

Studies propose that individuals who live in the Mediterranean zone or follow the Mediterranean diet have a lower danger of different infections, including weight, diabetes, malignant growth, and cardiovascular illness. They are additionally bound to appreciate a more extended life than individuals in different areas.

Key elements of the diet incorporate new foods grown from the ground, unsaturated fats, slick fish, a moderate admission of dairy, and a low utilization of meat and added sugar. Studies have connected these elements with positive wellbeing results.

Mediterranean Diet

Facts about the Mediterranean Diet

A diet routine that is acquiring in prevalence in numerous pieces of the world depends on the feasting practices of individuals that populate the Mediterranean district. Numerous individuals have known about the Mediterranean diet however are not especially acquainted with a portion of the particulars of the eating schedule.

To help you in getting more acquainted with the Mediterranean diet, a thought of eight valuable realities in regards to the components of this eating routine can be generally useful to you. Obviously, these are just some fundamental arguments about this important dieting schedule. Before you set out on such a diet plan, including the Mediterranean diet, you need to set aside the effort to talk with your doctor to verify that a proposed routine is suitable to your clinical status.

Eight interesting Facts about the Mediterranean Diet

The vital components of the Mediterranean diet are new products of the soil, entire grains, olive oil, fish, and wine with some restraint. As a result of this mix, the Mediterranean diet is one of the best dieting regimens to be discovered anyplace on the planet.

Meat and creature items are burned-through in limited quantities in the Mediterranean diet. Undoubtedly, when meat is incorporated inside the diet conspire; it is poultry or fish in by far most of cases.

Red meat is definitely not a staple in the Mediterranean diet and is seldom eaten by disciples to this dieting schedule. Individuals who really populate the nations around the Mediterranean Sea are once in a while seen eating red meats of any sort. Likewise, dairy items are utilized just sparingly inside the Mediterranean diet. For instance, if milk is remembered for a dinner or in the arrangement of food, it is of the low fat or non-fat assortment. Eggs are once in a while remembered for Mediterranean dinners. Without a doubt, a substantial egg -eater is one who has four eggs per week.

With the moderate utilization of fish, the Mediterranean diet permits followers an enormous wellspring of Omega-3 unsaturated fats. Examination has shown that a diet flush with Omega-3 unsaturated fats attempts to forestall coronary illness, stroke and even a few tumors.

Numerous ignorant individuals can be discovered offering the expression: "The Mediterranean diet simply isn't for me - it is excessively high in fat." In truth, the Mediterranean diet is high in particular sorts of fat. Upwards to 35 to a little less than half of the calories taken in through this diet do come from fat. Notwithstanding, the Mediterranean diet is strikingly low in immersed fat. It is immersed fat that has contrary results on an individual's wellbeing and prosperity.

The diet depends intensely on olive oil. (This is the essential motivation behind why the diet is higher in fat than one may expect.) Olive oil is demonstrated to build the degree of HDL cholesterol (otherwise called "great cholesterol").

The Mediterranean diet is incredibly high in cell reinforcements and fiber, two components that have been demonstrated to be useful in forestalling coronary illness and a few kinds of malignancy.

The dietary acts of the Mediterranean locale follow their birthplaces back to the times of the Roman Republic and the Roman Empire, starting in about the Fourth Century BC.

The Mediterranean diet was the fate of more global interest in present day times as right on time as 1945. A clinical specialist named Ancel Keys was answerable for empowering his own patients in the United States to go to the Mediterranean diet conspires. His support expanded the consciousness of the Mediterranean diet in different nations around the planet also.

Health Benefits of a Mediterranean diet

- A customary Mediterranean diet comprising of enormous amounts of new foods grown from the ground, nuts, fish, and olive oil—combined with active work—can lessen your danger of genuine mental and actual medical conditions by:

- **Forestalling coronary illness and strokes**. Following a Mediterranean diet restricts your admission of refined breads, handled nourishments, and red meat, and energizes drinking red wine rather than hard alcohol—all factors that can help forestall coronary illness and stroke.

- **Keeping you spry**. In case you're a more seasoned grown-up, the supplements acquired with a Mediterranean diet may diminish your danger of creating muscle shortcoming and different indications of delicacy by around 70%.

- **Lessening the danger of Alzheimer's**. Exploration proposes that the Mediterranean diet may improve cholesterol, glucose levels, and generally vein wellbeing, which thus may diminish your danger of Alzheimer's sickness or dementia.

- **Dividing the danger of Parkinson's infection.** The undeniable degrees of cell reinforcements in the Mediterranean diet can keep cells from going through a harming interaction called oxidative pressure, subsequently cutting the danger of Parkinson's infection fifty-fifty.

- **Expanding life span.** By lessening your danger of creating coronary illness or malignant growth with the Mediterranean diet, you're diminishing your danger of death at whatever stage in life by 20%.

- **Ensuring against type 2- diabetes**. A Mediterranean diet is wealthy in fiber which processes gradually, forestalls gigantic swings in glucose, and can assist you with keeping a healthy weight.

Tips:

- **Eat:** vegetables, organic products, nuts, seeds, vegetables, potatoes, entire grains, breads, spices, flavors, fish, fish and additional virgin olive oil.
- **Eat with some restraint**: Poultry, eggs, cheddar and yogurt.
- **Eat just infrequently**: Red meat.

Try not to eat: Sugar-improved refreshments, added sugars, prepared meat, refined grains, refined oils and other exceptionally handled nourishments.

Dodge These Unhealthy Foods

You ought to keep away from these unhealthy food sources and fixings:

- **Added sugar**: Soda, confections, frozen yogurt, table sugar and numerous others.
- **Refined grains**: White bread, pasta made with refined wheat, and so on
- **Tran's fats**: Found in margarine and different prepared food sources.
- **Refined oils**: Soybean oil, canola oil, cottonseed oil and others.

Prepared meat: Processed wieners, franks, and so forth

Exceptionally prepared food sources: Anything named "low-fat" or "diet" or which seems as though it was made in a manufacturing plant.

Nourishments to Eat

Precisely which nourishments have a place with the Mediterranean diet is disputable, incompletely on the grounds that there is such variety between various nations. The diet inspected by most examinations is high in healthy plant food sources and moderately low in creature nourishments.

Notwithstanding, eating fish and fish is suggested at any rate double seven days. The Mediterranean way of life likewise includes customary active work, offering dinners to others and getting a charge out of life. You should put together your diet with respect to these healthy, natural Mediterranean food sources:

- **Vegetables**: Tomatoes, broccoli, kale, spinach, onions, cauliflower, carrots, Brussels sprouts, cucumbers, and so on
- **Organic products**: Apples, bananas, oranges, pears, strawberries, grapes, dates, figs, melons, peaches, and so forth
- **Nuts and seeds**: Almonds, pecans, macadamia nuts, hazelnuts, cashews, sunflower seeds, pumpkin seeds, and so forth
- **Vegetables:** Beans, peas, lentils, beats, peanuts, chickpeas, and so forth.
- Tubers: Potatoes, yams, turnips, sweet potatoes, and so forth
- **Entire grains:** Whole oats, earthy colored rice, rye, grain, corn, buckwheat, entire wheat, entire grain bread and pasta.
- **Fish and fish:** Salmon, sardines, trout, fish, mackerel, shrimp, shellfish, mollusks, crab, mussels, and so forth
- **Poultry:** Chicken, duck, turkey, and so forth
- **Eggs:** Chicken, quail and duck eggs.
- **Dairy:** Cheese, yogurt, Greek yogurt, and so forth
- **Spices and flavors**: Garlic, basil, mint, rosemary, sage, nutmeg, cinnamon, pepper, and so forth

Healthy Fats: Extra virgin olive oil, olives, avocados and avocado oil.

What to Drink

Water ought to be your go-to drink on a Mediterranean diet. This diet additionally incorporates moderate measures of red wine around 1 glass each day. Nonetheless, this is totally discretionary, and wine ought to be dodged by anybody with liquor addiction or issues controlling their utilization.

Espresso and tea are additionally totally worthy, yet you ought to dodge sugar-improved drinks and organic product juices, which are high in sugar.

A Mediterranean Sample Menu for 1 Week

The following is an example menu for multi week on the Mediterranean diet. Don't hesitate to change the bits and food decisions dependent on your own necessities and inclinations.

Monday

- **Breakfast**: Greek yogurt with strawberries and oats.
- **Lunch**: Whole-grain sandwich with vegetables.
- **Supper**: A fish serving of mixed greens, wearing olive oil. A piece of organic product for dessert.

Tuesday

- **Breakfast:** Oatmeal with raisins.
- **Lunch**: Leftover fish serving of mixed greens from the prior night.

Supper: Salad with tomatoes, olives and feta cheddar.

Wednesday

- **Breakfast**: Omelet with veggies, tomatoes and onions. A piece of organic product.
- **Lunch:** Whole-grain sandwich, with cheddar and new vegetables.

Supper: Mediterranean lasagna.

Thursday

- **Breakfast:** Yogurt with cut leafy foods.
- **Lunch:** Leftover lasagna from the prior night.

Supper: Broiled salmon, presented with earthy colored rice and vegetables.

Friday

- **Breakfast**: Eggs and vegetables, seared in olive oil.
- **Lunch:** Greek yogurt with strawberries, oats and nuts.

Supper: Grilled sheep, with serving of mixed greens and heated potato.

Saturday

- **Breakfast**: Oatmeal with raisins, nuts and an apple.
- **Lunch:** Whole-grain sandwich with vegetables.

Supper: Mediterranean pizza made with entire wheat, finished off with cheddar, vegetables and olives.

Sunday

- **Breakfast:** Omelet with veggies and olives.
- **Lunch:** Leftover pizza from the prior night.
- **Supper**: Grilled chicken, with vegetables and a potato. Natural product for dessert.

Healthy Mediterranean Snacks

You don't have to eat multiple dinners each day. In any case, on the off chance that you become hungry between dinners, there are a lot of healthy nibble choices:

- A modest bunch of nuts.
- A piece of organic product.
- Carrots or child carrots.
- A few berries or grapes.
- Extras from the prior night.
- Greek yogurt.

Apple cuts with almond margarine.

A Simple Shopping List for the Diet

It is consistently a smart thought to shop at the border of the store. That is typically where the entire food sources are. Continuously attempt to pick the most un-handled alternative. Natural is ideal, however just on the off chance that you can undoubtedly bear the cost of it.

- **Vegetables**: Carrots, onions, broccoli, spinach, kale, garlic, and so on
- **Natural products:** Apples, bananas, oranges, grapes, and so forth
- **Berries:** Strawberries, blueberries, and so on
- **Frozen veggies:** Choose blends in with healthy vegetables.
- **Grains:** Whole-grain bread, entire grain pasta, and so on
- **Vegetables:** Lentils, beats, beans, and so on
- **Nuts:** Almonds, pecans, cashews, and so on
- **Seeds**: Sunflower seeds, pumpkin seeds, and so forth
- **Sauces**: Sea salt, pepper, turmeric, cinnamon, and so forth
- **Fish**: Salmon, sardines, mackerel, trout.
- Shrimp and shellfish.
- Potatoes and yams.
- Cheddar.
- Greek yogurt.
- Chicken.
- Fed or omega-3 enhanced eggs.
- Olives.

Extra virgin olive oil.

It's ideal to clear all unhealthy enticements from your home, including soft drinks, frozen yogurt, candy, baked goods, white bread, saltines and prepared food sources.

The Bottom Line

In spite of the fact that there isn't one characterized Mediterranean diet, this method of eating is for the most part wealthy in healthy plant food sources and generally lower in creature nourishments, with an emphasis on fish and fish. You can locate an entire universe of data about the Mediterranean diet on the web, and numerous extraordinary books have been expounded on it. Take a stab at go ogling "Mediterranean plans" and you will discover a huge load of extraordinary tips for heavenly suppers. By the day's end, the Mediterranean diet is inconceivably healthy and fulfilling. You will not be frustrated.

The Mediterranean diet Recipes

The following part of the book consists of the 70+ healthy and easy to make Mediterranean diet recipes which anyone can prepare at their home.

Breakfast Recipes

To follow the Mediterranean diet, you realize you ought to stack your plate with vegetables and useful for you proteins like salmon. Be that as it may, shouldn't something be said about breakfast? Natural product, dairy, and entire grains assume a major part in the diet, so there's in reality a great deal of delicious (and satisfying) breakfast alternatives to browse. Here are some delicious recipes to give you a go.

Spinach Artichoke Frittata

Frittatas have for quite some time been my go-to arrangement whenever I need to go through the dismal looking produce, shriveling spices, and little stubs of cheddar in my ice chest. Rarely do I make them with an arrangement up to this point.

Roused by my number one messy plunge and the warm spring climate, I concocted a frittata stacked with garlicky marinated artichoke hearts, hearty child spinach, pungent Parma, and rich harsh cream. I realized it would be acceptable, yet it blew away the entirety of my assumptions. Also, presently it's the lone frittata I need to make. In case you're not effectively all around familiar with it, you should realize that your supermarket's antipasti bar is fundamentally a secret stash of heavenly and helpful fixings.

Making a beeline for the antipasti bar is a specific must for this frittata, on the grounds that the marinated artichokes you'll discover there go about as the essential flavor promoter for your frittata. In contrast to their canned or frozen brethren, marinated artichokes are imbued with traces of garlic, spices, and appetizing olive oil that take this whenever egg dish from great to breathtaking.

Ingredients

- 10 huge eggs
- 1/2 cup full-fat harsh cream
- 1 tablespoon Dijon mustard
- 1 teaspoon fit salt
- 1/4 teaspoon newly ground dark pepper
- 1 cup ground Parmesan cheddar (around 3 ounces), separated
- 2 tablespoons olive oil
- Around 14 ounces marinated artichoke hearts, depleted, wiped off, and quartered
- 5 ounces child spinach (around 5 stuffed cups)
- 2 cloves garlic, minced

INSTRUCTIONS

- Orchestrate a rack in the broiler and warmth to 400°F.
- Spot the eggs, acrid cream, mustard, salt, pepper and 1/2 cup of the Parmesan in a huge bowl and speed to join; put in a safe spot.
- Warmth the oil in a 10-inch cast iron or broiler safe nonstick skillet over medium warmth until gleaming. Add the artichokes in a solitary layer and cook, blending at times, until daintily sautéed, 6 to 8 minutes. Add the spinach and garlic, and throw until the spinach is shriveled and practically the entirety of the fluid is vanished, around 2 minutes.
- Spread everything into an even layer. Pour the egg combination over the vegetables. Sprinkle with the excess 1/2 cup Parmesan. Slant the container to ensure the eggs settle equitably over all the vegetables. Cook undisturbed until the eggs at the edges of the dish start to set, 2 to 3 minutes.
- Prepare until the eggs are totally set, 12 to 15 minutes. To check, cut a little cut in the focal point of the frittata. In the event that crude eggs run into the cut, prepare for an additional couple of moments. Cool in the prospect minutes, at that point cut into wedges and serve warm.

1. Hearty Breakfast Fruit Salad

A seared grapefruit, a tasty smoothie bowl, or even a good smoothie is an enchanting method to begin quickly. In any case, some work day mornings require in excess of an organic product filled beginning, regardless of how yummy, to get your motors running and keep them running. You need something with protein and fiber, crammed with supplements; something quick that is fulfilling, energizing, and welcoming to start your motor. Here's another response to this predicament: a good entire grain and new natural product serving of mixed greens, with new spices that add measurement, and speedy sparkle of a sweet-tart dressing. It's totally made ahead and simply needs a very late throw together. This fruity tabouli is an equation, a formula outline that is so flexible you'll be having an alternate breakfast each day for quite a long time easily.

NGREDIENTS

For the grains:

- 1 cup pearl or hulled grain or any tough entire grain (see the rundown above)
- 3 cups water
- 3 tablespoons olive or vegetable oil, isolated
- 1/2 teaspoon legitimate salt
- For the natural product (see list above):

- 1/2 huge pineapple, stripped and cut into 1/2-to 2-inch lumps (2 to 2 1/2 cups)
- 6 medium tangerines or mandarins, or 5 huge oranges (around 1/2 pounds complete)
- 1/4 cups pomegranate seeds
- 1 little pack new mint

For the dressing:

- 1/3 cup nectar or another sugar (see list above)
- Juice and finely ground zing of 1 lemon (around 1/4 cup juice)
- Juice and finely ground zing of 2 limes (around 1/4 cup juice)
- 1/2 teaspoon legitimate salt
- 1/4 cup olive oil

1/4 cup toased hazelnut or nut oil

Equipment

- Estimating cups and spoons
- 2 rimmed preparing sheets
- Material paper
- Fine-network sifter
- Delicate silicone spatula
- 2 pots or 1 pan and a microwave-safe bowl
- Sharp blade
- 3 huge impenetrable holders with covers
- 2 more modest sealed shut compartments with covers
- 1 (3-cup) sealed shut compartment with a cover
- Blending bowl
- Wire whisk

Instructions

- **Wash the grain**: Line 2 rimmed preparing sheets with material paper. Flush the grain in a sifter under virus water until the water beneath is clear, around 1 moment. Delicately shake the sifter to deplete off any overabundance water. Spot the grain on one of the readied preparing sheets and utilize a spatula to spread out the grains into a solitary layer. Let dry totally, 3 to 5 minutes.

- **Warmth the water**: Warm the water on the burner or in the microwave; put in a safe spot.

- **Toast the grain**: Heat 2 tablespoons of the oil in a medium pot over high warmth until gleaming. Cautiously add the grain and toast, blending continually, until they simply start to obscure somewhat, 1 moment to 90 seconds.

- **Add the water:** Add the warm water and salt and heat to the point of boiling. Lessen the warmth to a stew or the least setting your burner has, cover, and cook until delicate and the vast majority of the fluid has been consumed, 40 to 45 minutes. Eliminate the pot from the warmth and let stand, covered, for 10 minutes, to allow the grain to steam and wrap up engrossing the water. In the meantime, prep the natural product, mint, and dressing.

- **Set up the organic product:** Place the pineapple lumps into one of the enormous compartments. Strip and cut the tangerines, mandarins, or oranges into fragments, eliminating as a large part of the severe white substance as possible. Spot in the compartment, cover, and refrigerate. Refrigerate the pomegranate seeds independently in a covered compartment.

- **Set up the mint:** Thinly cut or mince the mint leaves then refrigerate in its own covered holder.

- **Make the dressing:** Whisk the nectar, squeeze and flavors, and salt together in a medium bowl. Sprinkle in the olive oil, at that point the nut oil, while whisking continually until consolidated. Cover and refrigerate, or refrigerate in a container.

- **Dry and cool the grain**: Transfer the cooked grain onto the second arranged preparing sheet and spread into an even layer. Let cool totally, 10 to 20 minutes. Shower the grain with the leftover 1 tablespoon of oil and blend to cover.
- **Chill the cooked grain:** Transfer the grain to a huge holder, cover, and refrigerate.

Gather the plate of mixed greens and eat: To serve, scoop 2/3 cup of the grain into each bowl. Add around 6 bits of pineapple, 10 to 12 orange portions, and 1/4 cup pomegranate seeds into each bowl. Add 1 to 2 tablespoons of the mint and 2 to 3 tablespoons of the dressing to each bowl (re-whisk the dressing if necessary). Mix to blend and cover with the dressing.

2. The Best Shakshuka

- Shakshuka is a one-skillet dish of eggs poached in fragrant, spiced pureed tomatoes. In North Africa, Israel, and different pieces of the Middle East where it's discovered, it's frequently served for breakfast however it's generous enough to be delighted in any season of day, particularly when presented with pita or other bread to swipe up the sassy blend. It tends to be set up in various manners, and each form varies in its blend of flavors and aromatics. And keeping in mind that the tomato-based rendition is generally normal, there are numerous other flavorful translations (green shakshuka, for instance, is additionally worth difficult).

- In the event that you generally request shakshuka at your number one early lunch spot yet you've never attempted to make the dish at home, this formula is the absolute best spot to begin. The Middle Eastern egg dish has gotten fiercely well known, all things considered: It's incredibly soothing and pretty darn simple to make at home. Whenever you've taken in the couple of keys to progress, which we've laid out beneath, you'll be exceptional to make some extraordinary shakshuka at whatever point you need, regardless of whether for informal breakfast or a simple weeknight supper.

INGREDIENTS

- 1 (28-ounce) can entire stripped tomatoes
- 2 tablespoons olive oil
- 1 little yellow onion, finely hacked
- 2 tablespoons tomato glue
- 1 tablespoon harissa
- 3 cloves garlic, minced
- 1 teaspoon ground cumin
- 1/2 teaspoon genuine salt
- 6 huge eggs
- 1/4 cup approximately stuffed slashed new cilantro leaves and delicate stems
- 2 ounces feta cheddar, disintegrated (around 1/2 cup, discretionary)

  Hard bread or pita, for serving (discretionary)

- ## INSTRUCTIONS
- Pulverize the tomatoes. Pour the tomatoes and their juices into a huge bowl. Cautiously squash with your hands into scaled down pieces; put in a safe spot.
- Sauté the aromatics. Warmth the oil in a 10-or 12-inch skillet over medium warmth until shining. Add the onion and sauté until clear and mellowed, 5 to 6 minutes. Add the tomato glue, harissa, garlic, cumin, and salt, and sauté until fragrant, around 1 moment.
- Stew the pureed tomatoes for 10 minutes. Add the tomatoes and bring to a stew. Stew delicately until the sauce has thickened marginally, around 10 minutes.
- Break the eggs into the sauce. Eliminate the skillet from the warmth. Make 6 little wells in the sauce. Break an egg into each well.
- Spoon some sauce over the egg whites. Delicately spoon a touch of sauce over the egg whites, leaving the yolks uncovered (this will help the whites cook quicker so they set before the yolks). Cover and return the skillet to medium-low warmth.
- Cook the eggs 8 to 12 minutes. Cook, turning the dish depending on the situation with the goal that the eggs cook uniformly, until the whites are set and the yolks are to your ideal doneness, 8 to 12 minutes (keep an eye on it a couple of times). The eggs should in any case wiggle in the focuses when you delicately shake the skillet.
- Get done with cilantro and cheddar. Eliminate from the warmth. Sprinkle with the cilantro and feta, if utilizing, and present with bread or pita whenever wanted.

Balsamic Berries with Honey Yogurt

At the point when new berries are at their pinnacle mid-summer, I can't resist the urge to eat my weight in them. I sprinkle them onto my morning oats, eat them insane noontime, and appreciate them as a sweet yet healthy treat after supper. This snappy formula accepts the delicious summer leafy foods them into a quick and extravagant treat surprisingly fast. You may as of now have the ingredients in your kitchen at the present time, which implies this could be pastry tonight.t may appear to be strange to throw berries in vinegar for dessert, yet in the event that you've at any point attempted this mix, you realize how well it works. Balsamic vinegar, while tart, has a characteristic pleasantness to it.

At the point when showered over strawberries, blueberries, and raspberries, it draws a portion of the characteristic squeezes and sugars out of the natural product to make profoundly seasoned syrup for them to swim in. Much the same as that, the berries are an ideal method to cover off a dinner, however completing them with a spot of nectar improved yogurt certainly doesn't do any harm. Choose entire milk plain Greek yogurt for the smoothest lavishness.

INGREDIENTS

- 8 ounces strawberries, hulled and divided, or quartered if exceptionally enormous (around 1/2 cups)
- 1 cup blueberries
- 1 cup raspberries
- 1 tablespoon balsamic vinegar
- 2/3 cup entire milk plain Greek yogurt
- 2 teaspoons nectar

INSTRUCTIONS

Throw the strawberries, blueberries, and raspberries with the balsamic vinegar in an enormous bowl. Let it sit for 10 minutes. Mix the yogurt and nectar together in a little bowl. Split the berries between serving bowls or glasses and top each with a touch of nectar yogurt.

3. Caprese Avocado Toast

- With regards to avocado toast, the best cuts work out positively past two ingredients. On the off chance that you require additional verification, let us present this caprese avocado toast. All the segments of a caprese serving of mixed greens from the ready tomatoes and the smooth mozzarella to the new basil and the tart balsamic coating are an old buddy to the cool avocado. In the event that there was ever an illustration of when the entire is superior to the amount of its parts (and we're discussing powerful parts!), caprese avocado toast nails it on the head.

- While fat, round tomatoes and thick cuts of mozzarella are the stars of caprese serving of mixed greens, think more modest with regards to avocado toast. Stick with reduced down ingredients, similar to grape or cherry tomatoes and pearl-sized bundles of mozzarella.

INGREDIENTS

- 2 cuts generous sandwich bread, for example, worker bread, sourdough, entire wheat or multi-grain
- 1 medium avocado, split and pit eliminated
- 8 grape tomatoes, split
- 2 ounces new ciliegine or scaled down mozzarella balls (around 12)
- 4 huge new basil leaves, torn

2 tablespoons balsamic coating

INSTRUCTIONS

Toast the bread. While the bread is toasting, crush the avocado in a little bowl.

Spread the crushed avocado over the toast. Top each cut with tomatoes, mozzarella balls, and basil leaves, at that point sprinkle with balsamic coating. Serve right away

Spinach Feta Breakfast Wraps

Pre-winter, when fresh mornings cause me to disregard chilled for the time being oats and smoothies, and rather push warm morning meals to the front of my psyche. The lone test is finding warm morning meals that are still speedy enough to make on occupied fall mornings. Enter these cooler well-disposed breakfast wraps.

Following these tips for freezing burritos, I made veggie lover wraps loaded up with eggs, tomatoes, spinach, and feta that are prepared to microwave in the first part of the day. Skipping breakfast at Starbucks is much simpler when I can have this on my plate in just two minutes.

You could dress these wraps up with any fillings you'd like, yet I love this five-fixing variant enlivened by the wraps at Starbucks. This hits all the pivotal flavor focuses — exquisite eggs and spinach, pleasantly acidic tomatoes, and pungent feta cheddar — while remaining healthfully balanced. One of these wraps in addition to a hot mug of espresso, and I'm set until at any rate early afternoon.

INGREDIENTS

- 10 enormous eggs
- 1/2 pound (around 5 cups) infant spinach
- 4 entire wheat tortillas (around 9 creeps in width, burrito-sized)
- 1/2 16 ounces cherry or grape tomatoes, divided
- 4 ounces feta cheddar, disintegrated
- Margarine or olive oil
- Salt
- Pepper

INSTRUCTIONS

- In a huge bowl, whisk the eggs until the whites and yolks are totally joined. Spot an enormous skillet over medium warmth and add sufficient spread or olive oil to cover the base. At the point when the spread is liquefied or the oil is hot, pour in the eggs and mix infrequently until the eggs are cooked. Mix when there's no other option of salt and a liberal measure of dark pepper, at that point move to a huge plate to cool to room temperature.
- Wash or wipe down the skillet, place it back over medium warmth, and add another part of margarine or oil. Add the spinach and cook, blending frequently, until the spinach is simply shriveled. Spread the cooked spinach on another enormous plate to cool to room temperature.
- Organize a tortilla on a work surface. Add about a quarter every one of the eggs, spinach, tomatoes, and feta down the center of the tortilla and firmly wrap (perceive How to Wrap a Burrito). Rehash with the leftover three tortillas. Spot a couple envelops by a gallon zip-top pack and freeze until prepared to eat. In the event that freezing for over seven days, wrap the burritos in aluminum foil to forestall cooler consume. To warm, microwave on high for 2 minutes.
- Easy Homemade Muesli

- Muesli began in Switzerland by a doctor named Maximilian Bircher-Benner. His form, regularly alluded to as "Bircher muesli," comprised of whole oats, ground apples, and hacked nuts blended in with lemon squeeze, water, and improved consolidated milk. Today, muesli all the more regularly alludes to a blend of moved oats, nuts, seeds, and dried organic product. Consider it a better, low-sugar option in contrast to granola. Since muesli isn't prepared, there's no sugar or oil expected to tie the ingredients together despite the fact that I do get a kick out of the chance to toast the grains, nuts, and seeds before they're combined as one to draw out their flavors. It's additionally ideal to throw the grain with a warm flavor (like cinnamon, nutmeg, cardamom, cloves, or ginger) prior to toasting.

- Muesli checks all the cases of an ideal work day breakfast. You can make it ahead of time; it's loaded with entire grains, fiber, protein, and cell reinforcements; and it's very flexible, both by the way you cause it and how you to eat it. I like to make a major clump over the course of the end of the week to last consistently, which fundamentally accelerates my work day morning schedule. It's hot, nutty, chewy, and really fulfilling at last, a morning meal that can hold me until lunch.....Muesli can likewise be appreciated like cereal (on the off chance that I eat it along these lines, I top it with cut bananas or new berries), blended into yogurt, or heated up with milk or water and eaten like oats. To hold my morning meal routine back from feeling static, I like to change things up consistently. The adaptability additionally makes this a morning meal dish every one of my flat mates can concur on, in light of the fact that we've all discovered our #1 method to set it up. On the off chance that you do favor your morning meal on the better side, any of these arrangements can be done with a sprinkle of nectar or maple syrup, in spite of the fact that I locate a garnish of new organic product gives the perfect measure of pleasantness.

INGREDIENTS

- 3 1/2 cups moved oats
- 1/2 cup wheat grain
- 1/2 teaspoon legitimate salt
- 1/2 teaspoon ground cinnamon
- 1/2 cup cut almonds
- 1/4 cup crude walnuts, coarsely cleaved

- 1/4 cup crude pepitas (shelled pumpkin seeds)
- 1/2 cup unsweetened coconut chips
- 1/4 cup dried apricots, coarsely cleaved
- 1/4 cup dried cherries

INSTRUCTIONS

- Toast the grains, nuts, and seeds. Organize 2 racks to partition the stove into thirds and warmth to 350°F. Spot the oats, wheat grain, salt, and cinnamon on a rimmed preparing sheet; throw to join; and spread into an even layer. Spot the almonds, walnuts, and pepitas on a second rimmed heating sheet; throw to consolidate; and spread into an even layer. Move both preparing sheets to stove, setting oats on top rack and nuts on base. Prepare until nuts are fragrant, 10 to 12 minutes.

- Add the coconut. Eliminate the heating sheet with the nuts and put aside to cool. Sprinkle the coconut over the oats, get back to the upper rack, and prepare until the coconut is brilliant earthy colored, around 5 minutes more. Eliminate from broiler and put aside to cool, around 10 minutes.

- Move to an enormous bowl. Move the substance of both preparing sheets to an enormous bowl.

- Add the dried organic product. Add the apricots and cherries and throw to consolidate.

- Move to an impermeable compartment. Muesli can be put away in a hermetically sealed compartment at room temperature for as long as multi month.

- Appreciate as wanted. Appreciate as oats, grain, short-term oats, or with yogurt, finished off with new leafy foods sprinkle of nectar or maple syrup, whenever wanted.

4. Kale and Goat Cheese Frittata Cups

Frittatas are decent on the grounds that they're basic, and these frittata cups are easy to the point that they can sensibly advance into the work day arrangement.

While they are intended to be served warm, they're really magnificent room temperature or even cool, making them an incredible in and out lunch choice too. Furthermore, this formula is adaptable. Try not to like kale? Substitute an alternate verdant green. Have broccoli you need to go through? Cleave it up and toss it in. Lean toward Parmesan to goat cheddar? Forget about it. You can test here and discover an adaptation of this formula that suits your own taste.

In our home, frittatas, the Italian egg dish that is frequently made in a skillet, are typically saved for a Sunday clear out-the-cooler evening. They're easy to put together, fulfilling, and you can utilize practically any vegetable or cheddar you have available. In any case, of late, they've been advancing onto the morning meal table. All things considered, to be honest, I've been doing a compact adaptation for occupied work day mornings.

INGREDIENTS

2 cups hacked lacinato kale

- 1 garlic clove, daintily cut
- 3 tablespoons olive oil

- 1/4 teaspoon red pepper pieces
- 8 enormous eggs
- 1/4 teaspoon salt
- Run ground dark pepper
- 1/2 teaspoon dried thyme
- 1/4 cup goat cheddar, disintegrated

INSTRUCTIONS

- Preheat the broiler to 350°F. To get 2 cups kale, eliminate the leaves from the kale ribs. Wash and dry the leaves and cut them into 1/2-inch-wide strips.
- In a 10-inch nonstick skillet, cook the garlic in 1 tablespoon of oil over medium-high warmth for 30 seconds. Add the kale and red pepper chips and cook until withered, 1 to 2 minutes.
- In a medium bowl, beat the eggs with the salt and pepper. Add the kale and thyme to the egg blend.
- Utilizing a 12-cup biscuit tin, utilize the excess 2 tablespoons of oil to oil 8 of the cups (you may likewise utilize margarine or nonstick splash on the off chance that you'd like). Sprinkle the tops with goat cheddar. Prepare until they are set in the middle, around 25 to 30 minutes.
- Frittata is best eaten warm from the stove or inside the following day, yet extras can be kept refrigerated and warmed for as long as seven days.

- # Avocado and Egg Breakfast Pizza

- Presumably don't need to reveal to you that consolidating three of the world's most prominent nourishments gives you one fine breakfast: a warm round of chewy hull finished off with a splendid, cilantro-dotted avocado crush, and the ideal sloppy egg.
- I've generally had breakfast; however for a long time I stayed alive on cereal with milk, or toast with margarine and jam straightforward, carb-y suppers that normally left me a few hours after the fact. My propensities have changed and now my morning meals consistently incorporate an aiding of protein and fat alongside my carbs, which help to keep me fulfilled until noon. Avocados and eggs frequently show up, however not ordinarily on a similar plate. That is the thing that makes this formula exceptional.

INGREDIENTS

1 huge Hass avocado

- 1 tablespoon finely slashed cilantro
- 1/2 teaspoons lime juice
- 1/8 teaspoon salt
- 1/2 pound pizza batter, hand crafted or locally acquired (see Recipe Note)
- 4 huge eggs
- 1 tablespoon vegetable oil

Hot sauce, for serving (discretionary)

INSTRUCTIONS

Cut the avocado down the middle the long way, eliminate the pit and, with a huge spoon, scoop the tissue into a medium bowl. Add the cilantro, lime squeeze and salt. Crush with a fork until smooth, with a couple of pieces of avocado. Taste and change preparing. (Contingent upon the size of your avocado, you may require more salt or lime juice.) Set aside.

- Separation the mixture into 4 equivalent pieces. On an all-around floured cutting board, fold each piece into a dainty 6-inch circle. (In the event that the mixture continues to spring back as you move it, let it rest for a couple of moments to loosen up the gluten and attempt once more.)

- Warmth an all-around prepared cast iron skillet (see Recipe Note) over medium-high warmth until hot. Spot one of the mixture circles in the focal point of the skillet. Cook for 1 to 2 minutes, until the underside is sautéed and the top surface is bubbly. Flip and cook opposite side until seared, pushing down with a spatula if the batter puffs up off the lower part of the skillet. It could be burned in spots, which is fine. Move to a plate and rehash with outstanding batter circles.

- Spread 1/4 of the avocado combination onto each cooked piece of mixture.

- Warmth the oil in a skillet over medium warmth. (In the event that utilizing a similar skillet you utilized for the mixture, first let it cool somewhat and clear out any consumed flour that might be adhering to it.) Fry eggs to wanted doneness and spot everyone on top of a pizza. Serve quickly, with or without a sprinkle of hot sauce.

5. Smashed Egg Toasts with Herby Lemon   Yogurt

A completely cooked egg on hot buttered toast is, as far as I might be concerned, the stuff of dreams. Truth be told, I've basically gotten a specialist at hoisting the egg-on-toast combo. From frog in-the-opening to extravagant avocado toast and so on, I've made it.

My most recent redesign includes another most loved breakfast thing: yogurt! You'll begin by stirring up a flavorful Greek yogurt spread that is loaded with lemon and garlic, at that point spread it over the toast. Gently crush delicate bubbled eggs on top to make scraggly little pieces — they'll blend in with the yogurt and make an egg serving of mixed greens like combination that is smooth and rich. A light shower of olive oil and liberal topping of spices balance the entire thing, and unexpectedly the unassuming egg toast is a finished (and rich!) feast.

INGREDIENTS

- 8 huge eggs
- 1 clove garlic
- 1 medium lemon

- 2 tablespoons finely slashed new basil leaves, in addition to additional for embellish
- 2 tablespoons finely slashed new dill, in addition to additional for embellish
- 2 tablespoons finely hacked new chives, in addition to additional for embellish
- 2 cups plain Greek yogurt
- 2 tablespoons extra-virgin olive oil, in addition to additional for showering
- 3/4 teaspoon legitimate salt, in addition to additional for sprinkling
- 1/2 teaspoon newly ground dark pepper, in addition to additional for sprinkling
- 4 huge cuts country or sourdough bread (around 1-inch thick)

4 tablespoons unsalted spread, separated

INSTRUCTIONS

- Fill an enormous pot with around 5 creeps of water and bring to a turning bubble over high warmth; fill a huge bowl with cold water and ice. Lower the warmth until the water is at a quick stew. Tenderly lower 8 enormous eggs into the water each in turn. Bubble for precisely 6 minutes and 30 seconds. Utilizing an opened spoon, move the eggs to the ice shower. Let sit in the ice shower for 2 minutes, at that point strip the eggs under running water and put them in a safe spot.

- Set up the accompanying, adding them to a medium bowl: Mince 1 garlic clove. Finely grind the zing 1 medium lemon; at that point squeeze the lemon. Finely hack until you have 2 tablespoons new basil leaves, 2 tablespoons new dill, and 2 tablespoons new chives. Add 2 cups Greek yogurt, 2 tablespoons extra-virgin olive oil, 3/4 teaspoon fit salt, and 1/2 teaspoon dark pepper. Mix to consolidate.
- Cut 4 (1-inch thick) cuts dried up bread. Dissolve 2 tablespoons unsalted spread in an enormous skillet over medium warmth. Add 2 of the cuts and cook until brilliant earthy colored and fresh, around 2 minutes for each side. Move to a huge platter. Rehash with the excess 2 tablespoons unsalted margarine and bread.

Spread the yogurt blend on the bread; at that point top each toast with 2 of the eggs. Utilizing the rear of a spoon, delicately crush the eggs. Sprinkle with more genuine salt, dark pepper, and spices, and shower with more olive oil.

Lunch Recipes

Breakfast may be the main supper of the day, yet lunch is regularly the most ignored. Between picking the most straightforward alternative (cold extras!) and making the time amidst telecommuting (and possibly additionally "educating" kids), it's no big surprise we need that evening mug of espresso so seriously. In spite of your opinion, eating a sound, delightful lunch each day doesn't mean you need to commit your whole Sunday to supper prep, and we're here to demonstrate it. Continue to peruse for brisk lunch plans you can make very quickly.

Chickpea Pancakes With Greens and Cheese

These messy, green-y, and absolutely fulfilling chickpea hotcakes were roused by Healthyish benefactor Aliza Abarbanel's #1 work-from-home solace lunch. "I've filled these hotcakes with pretty much every extra in the cooler, from cooked greens to broiled mushrooms to marinated lentils, however melty cheddar stays a consistent," she says. Sans gluten and loaded with protein, chickpea flour flapjacks come in numerous varieties across the world, from Indian besan chilla to French socca to Italian farinata. In the event that you don't feel like or have the opportunity to make hotcake player during your mid-day break (however we energetically suggest it!) huge flour or alt-flour tortillas work superbly as a substitute; simply crease the cooked greens and cheddar inside the tortillas and warmth straightforwardly in the skillet to soften the cheddar.

Fixings

- 2 SERVINGS
- ½ cup chickpea flour
- 3 Tbsp. additionally 4 tsp. olive oil, separated
- Fit salt
- ½ medium red onion, meagerly cut
- 4 garlic cloves, crushed
- 1 cup brussels sprouts, meagerly cut
- little pack Tuscan kale or other kale, ribs and stems eliminated, meagerly cut
- tsp. hot sauce, in addition to additional for serving
- oz. sharp cheddar, coarsely ground
- Plain yogurt (for serving)

Arrangement

Stage 1

Preheat stove to 350°. Whisk chickpea flour and ½ cup in addition to 2 Tbsp. cold water in a little bowl. Rush in 1 Tbsp. oil and a touch of salt. Let sit at any rate 10 minutes and as long as 1 hour to permit flour to hydrate.

Stage 2

In the interim, heat 2 Tbsp. oil in a huge nonstick skillet over medium-high. Add onion, garlic, and brussels sprouts; cook, throwing sporadically, until mollified and softly seared, around 3 minutes. Add kale and cook, throwing frequently, until delicate, around 3 minutes. Add 2 tsp. hot sauce, season with salt, and throw well. Move to a medium bowl; clear out skillet.

Stage 3

Twirl 1 tsp. oil in skillet to cover; heat over medium-high. Empty ¼ cup hitter into focus of skillet and twirl to shape a dainty 6"– 7"- measurement flapjack. Cook until very much sautéed under and fresh around edges, around 2 minutes. Flip hotcake and cook just until second side is gently carmelized, around 1 moment. Move to a rimmed heating sheet. Rehash measure with residual player and 3 tsp. oil to make 4 aggregate. Split vegetables between 2 flapjacks and top with cheddar and staying 2 hotcakes. Heat until cheddar is liquefied, 6–8 minutes. Serve finished off with yogurt and more hot sauce.

Lunch Nachos With Spiced Cauliflower

Test Kitchen chief Chris Morocco depends on some adaptation of these lunch nachos in any event once every week as he conceptualizes what to take care of his two little youngsters. It's awesome to submit the recipe to memory: a pack of chips, a container of refried beans, perhaps some extra meat or simmered veg from the prior night, destroyed cheddar, and some sort of immediately cooked, spiced veg like cauliflower or brussels sprouts. It's a lightning-quick lunch (or supper) that can be changed to suit anybody's inclinations.

Fixings

2 SERVINGS

- 1 cup daintily cut radishes, red onion, cabbage, carrots, or other firm vegetable
- ½ cup prepared rice vinegar
- 3 Tbsp. extra-virgin olive oil, partitioned
- 2 garlic cloves, crushed
- ½ little head of cauliflower, divided through stem end, meagerly cut
- 1 tsp. ground coriander
- 1 tsp. ground cumin
- 1 tsp. paprika
- Genuine salt
- 8 oz. tortilla chips
- 1 cup refried beans (like Amy's)
- 8 oz. sharp cheddar, coarsely ground
- Cleaved avocado, cilantro leaves with delicate stems, and plain yogurt (for serving)

Readiness

Stage 1

Throw radishes and vinegar in a little bowl to consolidate; put in a safe spot.

Stage 2

Preheat stove to 400°. Warmth 2 Tbsp. oil in a huge skillet over medium-high. Cook garlic, throwing frequently, until brilliant around edges, around 2 minutes. Add cauliflower; cook, undisturbed, until brilliant earthy colored under, around 3 minutes. Throw, at that point keep on cooking, throwing infrequently, until seared all finished and fresh delicate, around 3 minutes more. Add coriander, cumin, paprika, and staying 1 Tbsp. oil. Cook, throwing, until fragrant, around 1 moment; season with salt.

Stage 3

Spread portion of chips on a little rimmed preparing sheet. Organize half of cauliflower on top. Bit half of beans over, at that point sprinkle with half of cheddar. Rehash layers once again. Prepare until cheddar is softened, 10–12 minutes. Top with depleted radishes, avocado, cilantro, and yogurt.

Broccoli Melts

Here's a working-from-home lunch that's quick enough to make between Zooms and will send you well on your way to meeting your daily veg quota. While there's something satisfying about the airy crustiness of a baguette, halved ciabatta rolls or slices of sourdough or whole wheat bread would work just as well.

Ingredients

2 SERVINGS

- 1small shallot or ¼ red onion, thinly sliced
- 1 Tbsp. plus 1½ tsp. sherry vinegar or red wine vinegar
- Pinch of sugar
- Kosher salt, freshly ground pepper
- 1small head of broccoli (8–10 oz.)
- 3Tbsp. extra-virgin olive oil
- 1garlic clove
- 2
- Tbsp. mayonnaise
- 1 tsp. hot chili sauce (such as Sriracha)
- 2 6" pieces baguette, halved lengthwise
- 4 slices sharp cheddar

Preparation

Step 1

Heat broiler. Combine shallot, vinegar, sugar, and a pinch of salt and pepper in a small bowl. Stir to combine; set aside.

Step 2

Trim and peel broccoli stem. Remove stem from crown and finely chop. Cut crown into florets, then coarsely chop into bite-size pieces.

Step 3

Heat oil in a large ovenproof skillet over medium-high. Add broccoli; season with salt. Cook, stirring occasionally, until browned in spots, about 3 minutes. Reduce heat to medium, add ¼ cup water, and cover. Cook until tender, about 2 minutes. Reduce heat to low and uncover. Grate in garlic; add reserved shallot mixture. Cook, stirring, until vinegar is mostly evaporated, about 15 seconds. Transfer to a bowl. Reserve skillet.

Step 4

Mix mayonnaise and chili sauce in a small bowl. Taste and add more chili sauce if desired.

Step 5

Broil bread, cut side up, in reserved skillet until lightly toasted, about 1 minute (watch carefully!). Remove from oven and spread mayo mixture over. Spoon broccoli mixture on top, going all the way to the edges (don't be afraid to pile it on). Drape a slice of cheese over (tear in half if needed).

Step 6

Broil, watching carefully, until cheese is bubbling and browned, about 3 minutes. Season with pepper.

Gyeran Mari

Gourmet expert Susan Kim offers Korean to-go lunch boxes loaded up with wonderfully arranged vegetables and different banchan, or little side dishes, through her NYC-based spring up Eat Doshi. We were so fascinated of these lovely doshirak that we requested that Kim show us how to reproduce a home-cooked adaptation that incorporates these appetizing moved egg omelet cuts loaded up with toasted kelp snacks and a mysterious fixing: Parm shavings. They're similarly acceptable delighted in all alone as a little bite, as a side dish to a bigger feast, or cut and presented with a bowl of rice. Kim utilizes sheets of toasted kelp snacks from brands like Seasnax or gimMe, which come pre-prepared with sesame oil and salt. Get the formula for the celery and turnip pickles, likewise highlighted in the container.

Fixings

- 2 - 4 SERVINGS
- 5 enormous eggs
- 2 Tbsp. mirin
- ½ tsp. white or customary soy sauce
- ½ tsp. genuine salt
- 1 Tbsp. vegetable oil
- 2 oz. Parmesan, shaved with a vegetable peeler
- 6 prepared toasted ocean growth snacks

Readiness

Stage 1

Whisk eggs, mirin, soy sauce, and salt in a 2-cup estimating glass. Warmth oil in a medium nonstick skillet over medium-low. Pour in 33% of egg blend, pivoting skillet to equally circulate. Cook until egg is generally cooked, around 1 moment. Dissipate 33% of Parmesan over and shingle 2 kelp snacks vertically down the middle. Utilizing an elastic spatula and beginning from one side, overlap egg over-top itself to move up firmly; push aside. Rehash cooking measure with half of outstanding egg combination, Parmesan, and ocean growth snacks, at that point flip existing egg turn over onto level egg and move up once more. Rehash once again with residual fixings. Move gyeran mari to a plate and let cool 5 minutes. Cut into ½"- thick pieces.

Tuna Salad With Crispy Chickpeas

Fish plate of mixed greens merits more than to be dolloped on dressed greens for lunch. Some seared chickpeas and the mash from endive improve things enormously.

Fixings

2 SERVINGS

- 5 Tbsp. extra-virgin olive oil, partitioned
- 1 15-oz. can chickpeas, flushed, wiped off
- Genuine salt
- 1 little shallot, finely cleaved
- 2 Tbsp. mayonnaise
- 1 Tbsp. Dijon mustard
- 1 Tbsp. red wine vinegar
- Newly ground dark pepper
- 1 5-oz. can water-stuffed fish, depleted
- 3 red or other endive, split transversely, leaves isolated
- ½ cup parsley leaves
- 2 Tbsp. (stacking) cut salted chiles
- ½ lemon

Readiness

Stage 1

Warmth 3 Tbsp. oil in an enormous skillet over medium-high. Cook chickpeas, throwing sometimes, until fresh and brilliant earthy colored, 6–8 minutes. Season with salt and let cool.

Stage 2

Whisk shallot, mayonnaise, mustard, and vinegar in a huge bowl; season dressing with salt and pepper. Blend in fish, saying a final farewell to a fork. Add chickpeas, endive, parsley, and salted chiles. Finely grind zing from lemon over, at that point press in juice. Pour in excess 2 Tbsp. oil and throw to consolidate. Taste and season with more salt if necessary.

Dinner Recipes

What would it be advisable for me to make for supper around evening time that is EASY? What are some acceptable, solid meals? Could I simply pay somebody to think of a simple supper thought for me? We're food bloggers—we in a real sense cook supper professionally—and these inquiries actually frequent us now and again. Remaining there, gazing into the ice chest, considering what you can prepare this evening that everybody will happily eat and that will not require a zillion hours—definitely, we've been there! For you (and for ourselves!) we've assembled this rundown of the 60 BEST, simple supper plans we have. They're everywhere—some are solid plans, some are somewhat more liberal, some are vegan plans, some are about a major piece of protein—yet they're brought together by their effortlessness. So here you have it! Our closest to perfect, simple suppers—across the board place.

- Broccoli Pesto Pasta. To make broccoli pesto, broccoli florets are whizzed right into the pesto sauce itself, adding an even more vibrant punch of emerald green to the sauce as well as a seriously healthy boost.
- Baked Salmon with Grapefruit Salad. Moist, flaky, melt-in-your-mouth salmon perfection. This is the easy salmon recipe you've been waiting for. Oh, and did we mention it cooks in just 15 minutes?
- Lemon Chicken. This easy recipe shines with a sunny, lemony zing. Garlic and herbs—plus a glut of white wine—mean that juicy, tender chicken breasts are as delicious as they are healthy.

<u>Ratatouille Sheet Pan Dinner With Sausage.</u>

While ratatouille is delicious served all on its own, we've added sausage to the mix to take this healthy sheet pan dinner to new heights.

<u>Salmon en Papillote.</u>

 Who knew that such an elegant meal could be so very easy.

<u>Instant Pot Chicken Marinara With Polenta.</u>

Our simple equation for this easy, satisfying dinner goes something like this: chicken thighs + a jar of marinara sauce = dinner's done.

Best, Easy Dinner Recipes For A Family

- <u>Sheet Pan Olive Bar Chicken</u>. Full of rich flavors, almost NO prep, and using only one pan, this dish is destined to become a new favorite.
- <u>Five Spice Chicken Sheet Pan Dinner</u>. Chicken thighs and cabbage get a little dose of flavor from Chinese five spice, and a little oven time on a sheet pan and boom! Dinner's done.
- <u>Sheet Pan Quesadilla with Jalapeño Ranch</u>. Stuffed with cheese and avocado, this giant, melty, upgraded cheese sheet pan quesadilla is good on its own, but we take it over the top with a side of homemade jalapeño ranch for dipping.
- <u>Instant Pot Mac and Cheese</u>. What's easier—and way better—than instant mac and cheese? Rich, creamy, homemade *Instant Pot* mac and cheese! Why? Because it takes about 5 minutes start-to-finish.

- Crock-Pot Chicken Taco Meat. Wait wait wait—taco night can be even easier? Yep! Meet our 3-ingredient Crock-Pot chicken taco meat recipe!

- Mango Chutney Chicken Sheet Pan. A jar of store-bought mango chutney is the secret to this ultra easy dinner.

- Old Bay Shrimp and Sausage Sheet Pan Dinner. Need we say more? Old Bay makes everything taste good—not that shrimp and sausage need any help.

- Za'atar Chicken Sheet Pan Dinner. We dressed up basic cauliflower and chicken with our latest favorite spice blend, za'atar.

Pork & Sausage Make Everything Taste AMAZING.

- <u>Sausage, Kale and Potato Skillet Dinner</u>. An easy one-pan sausage, kale and potato skillet that pleases everyone, from cook to clean-up crew.
- <u>Hoisin Glazed Pork Chops</u>. Having a few punchy ingredients on-hand is a great way to make a simple dinner out of just a few ingredients. Hoisin sauce is one of our go-to super-ingredients for easy dinners — just slather it on some pork chops, and you're well on your way to dinnertime bliss.
- <u>Pork Chops with Mushroom Cream Sauce</u>. Speaking of pork chops, this version — with a super creamy mushroom sauce — is ready in just 30 minutes.

- <u>Grilled Pork Tenderloin with Chimichurri</u>. Grilling always makes for an easy dinner, right? It's so fast, and the cleanup is minimal. Sliced up this pork tenderloin and serve it with a bowl of chimichurri—you'll be hearing raves for days.

- <u>Cauliflower Gnocchi with Bruschetta Sauce and Sausage</u>. This hearty, low-carb supper that bursts with bright, bold flavors and comes together in under ten minutes. It just doesn't get easier or healthier than that!

- <u>Sheet Pan Italian Sausage Heros with Honey Mustard</u>. The brilliant thing about breaking out your sheet pan to make italian sausage sandwiches with peppers is that it makes it so easy to make Italian hoagies for a crowd! Gather the hungry masses and let the feeding begin.

The Best Dinner Recipes of All Time Involve Steak— We Can All Agree on That, Right?

- <u>Grilled Rib Eye Steak with Italian Salsa Verde</u>. Easy? Check. Fast? Yup. Almost-no clean up? Uh, yeah, this recipe is perfect.

- <u>Carne Asada</u>. This easy carne asada recipe is as simple as can be—fire up the grill and you'll be feasting on juicy carne asada tacos in no time.

- <u>Chimichurri Steak</u>. For some reason, a perfectly grilled steak never fails to impress people. And it's really easy to do. Grab yourself about ten minutes, fire up the grill, and let's make a great steak!

- <u>Grilled Five Spice Flank Steak</u>. A Chinese five spice-hoisin marinade sinks into scored flank steak like nobody's business, and turns a simply grilled flank steak into a total flavor bomb.

Soup!

- <u>5-Ingredient Chicken Tortilla Soup</u>. As simple and easy as it sounds. No, actually, it's even easier than that.
- <u>Taco Soup</u>. Like tacos, but soup! Seriously!
- <u>Tikka Masala Soup</u>. Your favorite Indian chicken recipe, soup-ified.
- <u>Tortellini Soup with Italian Sausage and Kale</u>. Can we just call this "The Soup"? A creamy tomato base is loaded with cheese tortellini and hearty sausage and basically this soup is just the greatest dinner ever.

- <u>Quick and Easy Chicken Noodle Soup</u>. Just what it sounds like! Comfort in a pot.

- <u>Coconut Curry Ramen</u>. This restaurant-worthy creamy ramen is ready in about 15 minutes and is loaded with healthy veggies—in other words, it's a weeknight dream.

- <u>White Bean Soup with Bacon</u>. Creamy and deeply savory, it's hard to believe that this rich and hearty white bean soup with bacon is made from just five simple ingredients.

Oodles of Easy Noodle Recipes

- <u>Three-Ingredient Tomato Sauce</u>. Olive oil, salt, fresh tomatoes, and a little time are all it takes to create the most vibrant, fresh pasta sauce ever. Basic, easy, dinner perfection.

- <u>Creamy Roasted Red Pepper Pasta</u>. dinner doesn't get easier or more delicious than this creamy roasted red pepper rigatoni pasta. If you've got ten minutes and can open a jar, you can make this tonight.

- <u>4-Ingredient Stovetop Macaroni and Cheese</u>. Easy homemade mac and cheese is just ten minutes (and four ingredients!) away. So what are you waiting for?

- <u>Baked Gnocchi</u>. A skillet full of melty, bubbly, carb-y comfort is just what the dreary, drizzly weeknights ahead need to perk them up.

- <u>Baked Gnocchi with Broccoli</u>. A slightly healthier version, but just as cheesy, and just as easy.
- <u>Sesame Garlic Ramen Noodles</u>. Instant ramen noodles make this super simple dinner even faster.
- <u>Brown Butter Sage Cauliflower Gnocchi</u>. TJ's cauliflower gnocchi have literally never tasted so good.
- <u>Easy Bolognese</u>. Hearty and comforting, this meaty, easy bolognese sauce recipe takes less time to make than it does to disappear into hungry tummies.
- <u>Shrimp Scampi</u>. Buttery, garlicky, shrimp-y, and pasta-y (if you want it to be). Got 15 minutes? Great. Let's make shrimp scampi!

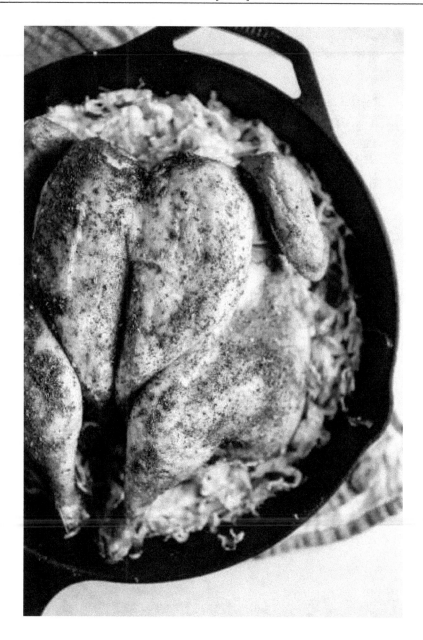

Dinner Ideas

Easy Harissa Chicken. Easy, quick harissa chicken—made with a jar of roasted red peppers, plenty of garlic, and smoked paprika—is a lot more exciting than any chicken recipe has any right to be.

- Cilantro-Lime Chicken Thighs. A quick marinade of lime, garlic, bright cilantro, and a touch of honey transforms boneless, skinless chicken thighs into just the juicy, tender surge of sunshine that you crave.
- Skillet Roasted Chicken with Cabbage. Easy delicious dinners win every time in our book. This one-pan whole roasted chicken falls into that easy category.
- Green Chicken Enchiladas. Our easy green chicken enchilada recipe is weeknight ready and all but guaranteed to please everyone from starving spouses to picky toddlers.

- <u>Perfect Roast Chicken with Lemon Herb Pan Sauce</u>. The original easy dinner — roast chicken. No sweat, no stress and GREAT leftovers. What's not to love?

- <u>Whole Roast Chicken with Carrots</u>. Same as above but with carrots! Um, yum.

- <u>Greek Chicken Freezer Meal</u>. Freezer meals are *future* easy meals, and this one is a real winner of a chicken dinner.

- <u>Freezer Chicken Fajitas</u>. Fajitas are easy anytime, but especially if you did most of the work a few months ago. Freezer meals FTW!

- <u>Chicken Piccata</u>. We just love recipes like this — not shortcuts required, because the classic recipe happens to be naturally fast and easy.

Stir-Fries: The OG Quick, Easy Dinner

- <u>Easy Orange Chicken</u>. Our easy orange chicken recipe puts a healthy spin on the sweet-savory favorite.
- <u>Kung Pao Chicken</u>. Step away from the takeout menu. Step towards the stove and make this easy chicken instead!
- <u>Thai Basil Beef</u>. A speedy, savory Thai beef basil stir fry that's just a bit spicy and really hits the spot.
- <u>Crispy Chicken Stir Fry</u>. Cornstarch and high heat mean super-crispy chicken every time. Toss in some green beans, and you've got an easy, healthy dinner in about 10 minutes.
- <u>Gingery Ground Beef (Soboro Donburi)</u>. Five ingredients, a few minutes and a hot skillet, and you'll be digging into a delicious soboro donburi.

Easy, Fast Vegetarian Dinner Ideas

- <u>Salsa Verde Baked Eggs</u>. A jar of salsa verde makes this elegant egg dish incredibly speedy. Yeah, it sounds brunchy, but trust us — try it for dinner!

- <u>Braised Chickpeas with Chard</u>. Rich, filling and healthy, this dinner is as fast and delicious as any we could imagine. Easy on the budget, too!

- <u>Portobello Mushroom Fajitas</u>. Just as good as their chicken or steak-filled counterparts, and just as fast, too.

- <u>Huevos Rancheros</u>. Runny, fried eggs over a bed of seasoned beans, atop a layer of warm corn tortillas, add a few condiments and voila — breakfast for dinner takes on a whole new meaning.

- <u>Soft-Scrambled Eggs</u>. Don't knock it — scrambled eggs make a perfect dinner in our book. Add a little salad if you want to round it out, and dinner will still be ready in about 10 minutes.

Desserts Recipes

A piece of what makes the Mediterranean diet so mainstream is the manner by which adaptable it is. You don't need to tally carbs or do any math to follow it. However long you're eating new foods grown from the ground with each supper, and picking entire grains over refined flours, you can enjoy different things.

Red meat is alright every so often, and you can eat fish and chicken a couple of times each week. The diet is normally high in plant-based protein from chickpeas, beans, and entire grains and you'll get a ton of your energy from sound fats and complex sugars that require a significant stretch of time to process.

Studies show this diet can do some incredible things for your wellbeing. That incorporates lower cholesterol, diminished danger for cardiovascular illness, and weight reduction. Obviously, there's no assurance you'll get these advantages, and there are alternate approaches to accomplish your wellbeing and wellness objectives other than restricting your diet to these nourishments. Indeed, the best wellbeing and wellness plan is the one that is nicely obliged the food sources you like to eat and the exercises you most appreciate.

Exacting diets can devour your day. What's more, from various perspectives, they can be similarly pretty much as undesirable as thoughtlessly or enthusiastically eating. All things considered, making little, insightful decisions for the duration of the day can improve your wellbeing without overwhelming your musings. Furthermore, that is the thing that this book is here for. We can help you structure an arrangement that leaves space for you to carry on with your life.

With this book, you get an individual wellbeing mentor who endeavors to help you make SMART objectives (that is Specific, Measurable, Attainable, Realistic and Time-situated) so you can remain persuaded all through the cycle. What's more, our caring local area gives you the help you need to remain on target. In the event that the correct diet for you incorporates some sugar – that is OK! We can represent that together. The Mediterranean diet is about balance, which implies dessert is not really impossible. Fixings like new organic product, olive oil, and yogurt are staples with regards to desserts, bringing about desserts that are light, new, and brimming with flavor. Like such a large amount of Mediterranean cooking, desserts are infrequently muddled, frequently meeting up in one bowl with only a couple fixings. Here are 10 of delicious and healthy Mediterranean dessert plans.

1. Blood Orange Olive Oil Cake

This cake is an ensemble of straightforward tastes additional virgin olive oil contributes a fruity nose, while a controlled measure of sugar clears a path for the pith of the blood orange, with its perplexing pleasantness and fragrant, clashing zing coming through in each nibble.

On the off chance that blood oranges aren't accessible, Cara or normal oranges make a pleasant substitute, since you'll be eating the whole natural product zing and all attempt to source natural citrus whenever the situation allows.

INGREDIENTS

- Cooking splash or extra-virgin olive oil
- 1 medium blood orange
- 1/4 cups generally useful flour
- 1/2 cup medium-crush cornmeal
- 2 teaspoons preparing powder
- 1/4 teaspoon preparing pop
- 1/4 teaspoon fine salt
- 2/3 cup in addition to 2 tablespoons granulated sugar, separated
- 1/2 cup entire milk plain yogurt
- 3 huge eggs
- 1/2 cup extra-virgin olive oil
- 4 paper-slim half-moon-formed blood orange cuts (discretionary)

INSTRUCTIONS

- Orchestrate a rack in the broiler and warmth to 350°F. Oil a 9-by 5-inch portion skillet with cooking splash or oil; put in a safe spot.

- Utilizing a vegetable peeler, eliminate the zing from the orange. Cut the zing into slender strips and put in a safe spot. Juice the orange and put aside 1/4 cup (save the leftover juice for utilization).

- Whisk the flour, cornmeal, heating powder, preparing pop, and salt together in a medium bowl; put in a safe spot.

- Whisk 2/3 cup of the sugar and the 1/4 cup blood orange squeeze together in enormous bowl. Each in turn, speeds in the yogurt, eggs, and olive oil. Whisk the flour combination into the wet ingredients, giving the blend 20 great turns with the speed until just joined. Overlap in the zing strips.

- Move the hitter into the readied skillet. Top with the blood orange cuts and staying 2 tablespoons sugar. Heat until the top is springy and brilliant earthy colored, and a wooden stick embedded in the middle comes out with only a couple morsels joined, 50 to an hour.

Allow the cake to cool in the dish on a wire rack for 20 minutes. Cautiously unmold the cake, flip it back to be straight up, and get back to the rack to cool totally.

Balsamic Berries with Honey Yogurt

It might appear to be nonsensical to throw berries in vinegar for dessert; however in the event that you've at any point attempted this mix, you realize how well it works. Balsamic vinegar, while tart, has a characteristic pleasantness to it. At the point when showered over strawberries, blueberries, and raspberries, it draws a portion of the normal squeezes and sugars out of the natural product to make profoundly seasoned syrup for them to swim in. Much the same as that, the berries are an ideal method to cover off a dinner, however completing them with a touch of nectar improved yogurt certainly doesn't do any harm. Select entire milk plain Greek yogurt for the most velvety lavishness.

INGREDIENTS

- 8 ounces strawberries, hulled and split, or quartered if extremely enormous (around 1/2 cups)
- 1 cup blueberries
- 1 cup raspberries
- 1 tablespoon balsamic vinegar
- 2/3 cup entire milk plain Greek yogurt

2 teaspoons nectar

INSTRUCTIONS

Throw the strawberries, blueberries, and raspberries with the balsamic vinegar in a huge bowl. Let it sit for 10 minutes. Mix the yogurt and nectar together in a little bowl. Split the berries between serving bowls or glasses and top each with a spot of nectar yogurt.

Sticky Gluten-Free Lemon Cake

Warm cake and warm syrup are the things that make this lemony cake so sodden and tasty. Ensure you jab a lot of openings in the cake so the syrup gets an opportunity to douse into each and every nibble of cake as it cools. I realize it'll be difficult to be persistent, however stand by until the cake cools totally with the goal that all the flavors truly get an opportunity to merge and you'll be remunerated. This cake is heated in a spring structure search for gold evacuation for cutting (when the syrup goes on, it's difficult to eliminate from the container in one piece). You can positively make it in a normal cake dish, yet it will presumably be ideal to cut and teach it a thing or two out of the container. This cake is incredible all alone, yet stunningly better with a touch of frothy whipped cream on top!

INGREDIENTS

For the cake:

- 2 cups almond flour
- 3/4 cup polenta
- 1/2 teaspoons heating powder
- 1/4 teaspoon salt
- 14 tablespoons (7 ounces) unsalted margarine, at room temperature, in addition to additional for the skillet
- 1 cup granulated sugar
- 3 enormous eggs
- Finely ground zing of 2 medium lemons
- 1/2 teaspoon vanilla concentrate

For the syrup and serving:

- 1/2 cup powdered sugar
- 3 tablespoons newly crushed lemon juice
- Whipped cream, for serving (discretionary)

INSTRUCTIONS

For cake:

- Organize a rack in the stove and warmth to 350°F. Line the lower part of a 9-inch spring form skillet with material paper. Coat the paper and sides of the container with margarine; put in a safe spot.
- Spot the almond flour, polenta, heating powder, and salt in a medium bowl and race to consolidate; put in a safe spot.
- Spot the margarine and sugar in the bowl of a stand blender fitted with the oar connection. (Then again, utilize an electric hand blender and huge bowl.) Beat on medium speed until helped in shading, around 3 minutes.
- With the blender on medium speed, add 1/3 of the almond flour combination and beat until fused. Beat in 1 egg until consolidated. Keep beating in and substituting the leftover almond flour blend and eggs in 2

additional options. Stop the blender and scratch down the sides of the bowl with an elastic spatula.

- Add the lemon zing and vanilla concentrate and beat until just consolidated. Move the hitter to the container and spread into an even layer.

Heat until the edges of the cake has started to pull away from the sides of the skillet, around 40 minutes. Spot the skillet on a wire rack and make the syrup.

For the syrup:

- Spot the powdered sugar and lemon juice in a little pot over low warmth and cook, mixing periodically, until the powdered sugar is totally broken up and the syrup is warm. Eliminate from the warmth.
- Utilizing a toothpick, punch holes everywhere on the cake, dispersing the openings around 1-inch separated. Gradually shower the warm syrup uniformly over the cake. Allow the cake to cool totally, around 1/2 hours. Eliminate the sides of the skillet, cut into wedges, and present with whipped cream whenever wanted.

2. Honeyed Phyllo Stacks with Pistachios, Spiced Fruit & Yogurt

- One of the old adages of evening gatherings is this: Do not cause a recipe interestingly when you to have visitors coming over. However, a few recipes are an exemption, similar to this one, which I tried interestingly on a full table of visitors. They cherished its layers of shatteringly fresh phyllo, the light whirls of yogurt, and the filling of hacked raisins, nectar, and pistachios rather like a lighter, deconstructed baklava.

- Here's something intriguing about phyllo, as well: I gained from one of our perusers that phyllo batter is really vegetarian it's made with oil, not spread. This adaptable cooler staple is additionally an accommodating part for amassing liked up desserts that look wonderful yet are really a snap to make, similar to this one. You can make little cakes with the batter, as we do here and even layer them with delicate cheddar, safeguarded natural product, and sweet-smelling nectar. Or on the other hand you can proceed to make a veggie lover dessert by avoiding the dairy yogurt and utilizing coconut yogurt all things considered, and subbing agave, earthy colored rice syrup, or sorghum syrup for the nectar.

INGREDIENTS

For the phyllo mixture:

- 6 sheets phyllo mixture, defrosted
- 1/4 cup sugar
- 1/4 teaspoon ground cinnamon
- 1/4 cup extra-virgin olive oil
- For the pistachio and organic product blend:
- Zing and juice of 1 orange (around 1/4 cup juice)
- 2 tablespoons sugar
- 2 tablespoons nectar
- 1/2 cup dried brilliant raisins, generally cleaved
- 1 cup cooked unsalted pistachio nuts, generally cleaved
- 1/2 cup pitted dates, generally cleaved
- 1/2 teaspoon ground cardamom
- **For yogurt:**
- 1 cup entire milk Greek yogurt
- 1 tablespoon confectioners' sugar
- Zing of 1 lemon
- **For serving:**
- 1/2 cup pomegranate arils

- 1/4 cup pistachios, cleaved
- Nectar, warmed
- Raspberries or strawberries to decorate, discretionary
-

INSTRUCTIONS

To set up the phyllo squares:

Preheat the broiler to 400°F and fix an enormous preparing sheet with
  material.

- Stack the phyllo sheets on the ledge and cover freely with a scarcely soggy towel. Join the sugar and cinnamon in a little bowl. Put the oil in another little bowl. Eliminate a sheet of phyllo and spot it on the readied preparing sheet. Utilizing a cake brush, gently cover the phyllo mixture with the olive oil and sprinkle softly with the cinnamon sugar. Top with another sheet of phyllo, oil, and cinnamon sugar. Rehash with the entirety of the sheets, yet when you get to the top layer, brushes it gently with oil. Use kitchen shears to clip the layered mixture into 12 squares or square shapes of equivalent size.

- Heat the phyllo batter for 7 to 8 minutes or until it is brilliant earthy colored and fresh. Allow it to cool totally. The readied phyllo squares can be put away in a water/air proof holder at room temperature for as long as 3 days.

- **For pistachio and fruit mix:**

- In a little pot, heat the orange zing and orange squeeze, sugar, and nectar until the juice boils and the nectar breaks down. Mix in the brilliant raisins and put the dish in a safe spot.

Blend the pistachios in with the dates. Mix in the cardamom. Mix the spiced pistachios and dates into the container with the syrup and raisins. Put aside the pistachio and organic product blend to marinate for in any event 30 minutes. This combination can be made as long as 5 days early and put away in the fridge.

For yogurt:

Altogether blend the yogurt in with the confectioners' sugar and lemon zing. The yogurt combination can be refrigerated for as long as 5 days, all around covered.

For dessert:

- Smear around 1 tablespoon of yogurt on a phyllo cake square. Spot on an individual dessert plate. Top with a liberal spoonful of the organic product combination, at that point another phyllo square. Rehash, and top with a last cake square and a little dab of yogurt. Sprinkle the stack and the dish around it with pomegranate arils and pistachios; at that point shower delicately with warmed nectar. Rehash, making 4 phyllo square stacks, and serve right away. Enhancement whenever wanted with occasional organic product like raspberries or strawberries.

Fig and pistachio cake

You don't have to roast them; they are a perfectly fine accompaniment on their own. But the thought of honey-scented figs just upped the autumn factor for me. They are also really good by themselves, if you don't have time to make a cake. Pistachios ready for pulverizing. The cake is essentially a Genoese, made nutty with pistachios and moistened with sugar syrup. I found the mascarpone cream had a weight and tang that contrasted nicely with the light sponge cake, more so than just a basic whipped cream filling. I also didn't want to make the cake too sweet, as the figs-and-honey was already providing plenty of sweetness.

Ingredients

For pistachio cake

- 40 g pistachios
- 75 g powdered sugar
- 40 g blanched almonds
- 40 g egg yolks
- 60 g eggs
- 115 g egg whites
- 2 g cream of tartar
- 50 g + 1/2 cup sugar
- 60 g all-purpose flour

For mascarpone frosting

- 1 cup heavy cream
- 8 oz. mascarpone cheese
- 1/2 cup powdered sugar

For roasted figs

- About 12 ripe figs
- 1 tablespoon unsalted butter
- 2 tablespoons honey

Instructions

For the cake:

- Preheat oven to 425 degrees F. Grease two 8x8 pans, line with parchment paper, and grease parchment paper.
- Combine pistachios, powdered sugar, and almonds in a food processor. Process until nuts are finely ground.
- Pour nut mixture into a large mixing bowl. Add in eggs and egg yolks and stir until combined.
- Combine egg whites, cream of tartar, and 2 tablespoons of the 50 g of sugar in bowl of a stand mixer. Whip until soft peaks form. Add remaining sugar and whisk until stiff peaks.
- Sift the flour over the nut mixture and stir to combine. Add in the egg whites and carefully fold in.
- Divide the batter between the two pans. Bake for 8-10 minutes until the tops are lightly colored and the top just springs back to the touch.

Remove from oven and place on wire racks. Run an offset spatula or knife around the edges to loosen the cake from the pans. Let cool.

- For the sugar syrup: Combine the remaining 1/2 cup sugar and 1/2 cup water in a medium saucepan on the stove and bring to a boil, stirring to let the sugar dissolve. Let cool.

For mascarpone frosting:

- Combine all ingredients in bowl of a stand mixer. Whisk together until soft peaks form. Add more confectioner's sugar if you would like it sweeter. Do not over whisk or the mixture will curdle.
- To assemble the cake: Trim off the edges of each square of edge to even them off. Place one layer of cake on a plate. Brush a little of sugar syrup over the cake layer. Spread a layer of frosting evenly on top. Place second layer of cake on frosting and brush sugar syrup over it. Spread a layer of frosting evenly on top.
- Refrigerate cake for about an hour or so to let frosting set. When you are ready to serve the cake, you can take it out and trim the sides so they look nice and even.

For the figs:

- Preheat oven to 425 degrees F. Wash figs and slice them in half. Arrange in an ovenproof baking dish just large enough to fit them.
- Combine butter and honey in a small saucepan and cook over medium heat on the stove until butter is melted. Pour over the figs.
- Place figs in oven and bake for about 13-15 minutes, until the sauce is bubbling. Remove figs and let cool on wire rack for a few minutes before serving.

Vegan Chocolate Chip Cookies

Ingredients:

- 2 cup all-purpose flour
- 1 tsp. baking soda
- 1/2 tsp. kosher salt
- 1/2 cup dark brown sugar
- 1/2 cup granulated sugar
- 1/2 cup canola oil
- 1/4 cup water
- 2 tsp. pure vanilla extract
- 1 cup bittersweet chocolate chips

1 cup semisweet chocolate chips

Instructions

- In a bowl, mix salt, baking soda, and flour. Toss with chocolate. In another bowl, break up brown sugar, making sure there are no lumps. Add granulated sugar, oil, water, and vanilla and whisk to combine. Add flour mixture and mix until just completely mixed (there should be no streaks of flour). Put two cookie sheets with parchment paper. Spoon out 2-inch mounds of dough, spacing 2 inches apart. Freeze 30 minutes.

Preheat oven to 375°F. Bake cookies, rotating position of pans after 6 minutes until edges are golden brown, 9 to 12 minutes total. Let cool.

Cinnamon Walnut Apple Cake Baked with Olive Oil

We utilize olive oil for everything, including heating desserts (Mediterranean Diet recipes traditionally utilize olive oil for preparing). This cinnamon pecan apple cake has been heated for exceptional events in my family for ages. Despite the fact that we have natural product for dessert on most evenings, we will make this as a treat when we are celebrating. Olive oil makes for smooth and clammy prepared merchandise and I would energetically suggest it for the vast majority of your heating needs. One tip is to attempt to get a rich or fruity enhanced olive oil when you are heating. Eat this cake with evening tea or espresso or after a quick bite.

Ingredients

- 4 eggs
- 1 cup earthy colored sugar (in addition to 2 Tablespoons for apples)
- 1 cup additional virgin olive oil
- 1 cup milk
- 2 1/2 cups wheat flour
- 2 teaspoons preparing powder
- 1 teaspoon vanilla concentrate
- 4 apples, stripped, split, cored, and daintily cut

- 1/2 cup pecans, cleaved
- 1/2 cup raisins
- 1/2 teaspoons ground cinnamon

3 tablespoons sesame seeds

Instructions

- Preheat stove to 375 degrees.
- Beat eggs and sugar with a hand blender for 10 minutes. Add olive oil and beat for an extra 3 minutes.
- Add milk, wheat flour, preparing powder and vanilla. Beat for 2 minutes.
- Brush a 9" cake container with olive oil. Add a large portion of the hitter to the skillet.
- In a bowl, blend apples, 2 tablespoons of earthy colored sugar, pecans, raisins and cinnamon. Pour apple combination on top of hitter in cake skillet.
- Add remaining hitter to container and sprinkle with sesame seeds.
- Heat for 45-50 minutes until embedded blade confesses all.

3. Vanilla Cake Bites

Ingredients:

- 1 1/4 cups Medjool dates

- 1 1/4 cups raw walnuts

- 1 cup almond flour

- 1/3 cup coconut flour

- Pinch sea salt

- Two teaspoon vanilla extract

Finely shredded unsweetened coconut *(optional)*

Intructions

- Pulse pitted dates in a food processor until small bits remain. Take it out from the food processor and placed it apart. Add the almond flour, walnuts, coconut flour, and sea salt into the food processor. Blend till a semi-high-quality meal is carried out. Add dates returned in addition to the vanilla extract. Pulse until loose dough form. Be careful not to over-blend. You're looking for pliable dough, not a purée. Using a cookie scooper, scoop out 2-Tablespoon amounts and roll into balls with hands or release lever on the scoop and place directly on a parchment-lined baking sheet. Repeat until all dough is used up. Roll in finely shredded coconut, or leave it as is. Store in refrigerator or freezer. Keep in the fridge for up to 6-7 days or in the freezer for up to 3-4 weeks. You can also make a loaf from the dough or 6×6-inch cake pan and slice it into bars.

GREEK YOGURT CHOCOLATE MOUSSE

Chocolate Mousse must be a definitive in enticing dessert recipes. Rich and chocolaty there is something just so fulfilling about it. In any case, given that it's made with a tone of twofold cream and frequently a hill of refined white sugar additionally, it's not the best choice out there so I set about making it somewhat better for us. Conventional chocolate mousse additionally contains crude eggs. I wasn't excited about offering this to the child so I needed to likewise make a rendition that was sans egg. Without the whipped cream and eggs this mousse will not interpretation of that trademark light and vaporous surface.

INGREDIENTS

- 180ml/3/4 cup milk
- 100g/3 1/2 oz dull chocolate
- 500ml/2 cups greek yogurt
- 1 tbsp nectar or maple syrup

1/2 tsp vanilla concentrate

INSTRUCTIONS

- Empty the milk into a pot and add the chocolate, either ground or finely cleaved or shaved. Tenderly warmth the milk until the chocolate softens, being mindful so as not to allow it to boil. When the chocolate and milk have completely joined, add the nectar and vanilla concentrate and blend well.
- Spoon the greek yogurt into a huge bowl and pour the chocolate blend on top. Combine as one well prior to moving to singular dishes, ramekins or glasses.
- Chill in the ice chest for 2 hours. Present with a little spoonful of greek yogurt and some new raspberries.
- The chocolate mousse will keep in the cooler for 2 days.

Peanut Butter Protein Balls

Ingredients

- 1 cup large Medjool dates pitted

- 2-4 tablespoons water

- 1 cup peanut flour

- 3/4 cup oats

- 1/2 cup roasted peanuts

- 1/4 cup natural peanut butter

- 2 tablespoons flax seeds ground into meal

- pinch of salt

- 1/4 cup chocolate chips optional

Instructions

Put the pitted dates in about 2 cups of water for 25- 30 minutes. Drain, reserving the water. In a food processor combination dates with 2-four tablespoons of water, slowly adding water as wanted and scraping down the edges frequently till a paste has formed. Add peanut butter, peanuts, salt, flax seeds, peanut flour, and oats and blend together into a thick dough. Round out about 2 tbsp. of dough into balls and place on a parchment-lined baking sheet. Refrigerate for 1 hour until firm. Store in an airtight container in refrigerator up to 5 days or in the freezer for 1 month.

CPSIA information can be obtained
at www.ICGtesting.com
Printed in the USA
BVHW051532260321
603512BV00012BA/1287